THE
MOUND
BUILDERS

THE MOUND BUILDERS

A play by Lanford Wilson

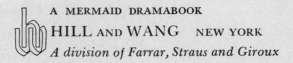

A MERMAID DRAMABOOK

HILL AND WANG   NEW YORK

A division of Farrar, Straus and Giroux

Library of Congress Cataloging in Publication Data

Wilson, Lanford, 1938–
The mound builders.
(A Mermaid dramabook)
I. Title.
PS3573.1458M6   812'.5'4   76-18235
ISBN 0-8090-7104-5
ISBN 0-8090-1235-9 pbk.

For Roy London

THE MOUND BUILDERS was first presented by the Circle Repertory Company in New York City on February 2, 1975. It was directed by Marshall W. Mason with the following cast:

PROFESSOR AUGUST HOWE	*Robert Thirkield*
CYNTHIA HOWE	*Stephanie Gordon*
KIRSTEN	*Lauren S. Jacobs*
D. K. ERIKSEN	*Tanya Berezin*
DR. DAN LOGGINS	*Jonathan Hogan*
DR. JEAN LOGGINS	*Trish Hawkins*
CHAD JASKER	*John Strasberg*

The set was by John Lee Beatty, costumes by Jennifer von Mayrhauser, sound by Charles London and George Hansen, slides by Charles London and Robert Thirkield. The production stage manager was Peter Schneider.

The author expresses his thanks to the Rockefeller Foundation for support during the writing of this play, and to Dennis Logan Schneider and Marlyn Baum for their assistance in the research, and especially to Dr. Howard Winters of the Department of Anthropology, New York University, who kindly helped with the archaeological data, spoke with the cast and production crew of THE MOUND BUILDERS, *and generously gave us a hint at an archaeologist's dream.*

THE
MOUND
BUILDERS

CHARACTERS

PROFESSOR AUGUST HOWE, an archaeologist, forty

CYNTHIA HOWE, his wife, thirty-five

KIRSTEN, his daughter, eleven

D. K. (DELIA) ERIKSEN, his sister, thirty-eight

DR. DAN LOGGINS, his assistant, an archaeologist, twenty-nine

DR. JEAN LOGGINS, Dan's wife, a gynecologist, twenty-five

CHAD JASKER, the landowner's son, twenty-five

THE SCENE

AUGUST's *study in Urbana is indicated only by a desk or table that can be easily incorporated into the house at Blue Shoals. When* AUGUST *is alone, the lights confine us to his immediate desk area. From this light he wanders, while recording, off into the dark, and back again, sitting, standing, messing with things on his desk.*

As we move into the previous summer, the house around him is revealed: An old farmhouse with a large living-dining room transformed into a living-dining-working area by the archaeologists. A stairway leads off to the bedrooms, a door opens to AUGUST's *office, doors lead to an unseen front porch and a back porch that might be incorporated into the set and used as a playing area for a number of the scenes. An arch allows us to see part of the kitchen, in which there is a refrigerator.*

The back wall of the set serves as a screen onto which are back-projected slides from the previous summer that serve AUGUST *as the backbone of his recorded notes. He need not literally control the projector.*

The house is seen from AUGUST's *memory of the wrecked expedition and may be represented as he sees it—not in photographs but in his mind's eye: a house that lifted up like an ark as the lake flooded the valley and floated down some great flood-struck current, wrecking in another place.*

Scenes in the house are accompanied by a dense orchestration of the outside sounds, opening the house onto its surroundings. The night is filled with noises of the country and the day with the sounds of bulldozers and workmen preparing the lakebed, which will flood the valley.

THE TIME

February in Urbana and the previous summer in Blue Shoals, Illinois—located in the extreme south of that state, in the five-state area of Kentucky, Missouri, Indiana, Arkansas, and Illinois—at the confluence of the Wabash, Cumberland, Ohio, and Mississippi Rivers.

ACT 1

AUGUST

(Sits at a desk, speaking into the microphone of a small tape recorder.)
One, two, three, four, five . . . *(Getting up, walking a few paces away.)* The quick gray fox jumped over . . . whatever it was the quick gray fox jumped over. *(He returns to the desk, clicks off the tape, rewinds it, and clicks it on. We hear his voice repeating ". . . three, four, five . . . the quick gray fox jumped—" He clicks the machine off, then back to record.)* Dianne . . . ah . . . good morning. Or, knowing your habits, I should probably say, Good afternoon. *(Pause. He walks away a few paces.)* After months of procrastination, with which I'm sure you're sympathetic, I intend to go through what is left of the wreckage of last summer's expedition. *(He returns to the desk.)* You may type this up, or go out to lunch. I'll understand either. *(He touches something on the desk. The back screen is filled with a scenic photograph of a lake at morning.)* This is the lake, against which we were racing time. *(Slide: the house.)* This is the house in which we were staying. After we spent three summers of excavation *(Slide: dam construction.)* on the mounds—within earshot of the construction of the Blue Shoals Dam— *(Slide: bulldozer.)* Engineers preparing the lake bed— *(Slide: the dig.)* uncovered evidence of an extensive village site not six hundred yards from the front door *(Several slides lead us past the lake-bed construction to the house, as we hear a car stopping outside, doors slamming, and the lights of the*

stage begin to reveal the house in Blue Shoals.) of the
house in which we stayed. Excavation of the Jasker Village
site was a salvage operation undertaken literally as the
lake basin filled behind us.

CYNTHIA
(*Coming down the stairs, followed by* KIRSTEN.)
God, I thought they'd never get here. They must have
come through Blue Shoals.
(*She goes to the door.*)

CHAD
(*Off*)
Window's been opened for a week, I was telling the professor we had a hell of a spring. Thought it wasn't gonna be
any good for you folks, but it's dried up the last week.

AUGUST
Thank God you're here. (*As* DAN, CHAD, *and* JEAN *enter,
carrying luggage, etc.*) Everything possible has conspired
to work against us.

DAN
Girls getting to you?

AUGUST
I'm going to have to go to the Paducah airport. How far is
Paducah?

CYNTHIA
If there is such a place.

CHAD
About an hour.

CYNTHIA
Auggie's sister is being dumped on us.

AUGUST

It's nothing to talk about; just one more thing.

CYNTHIA

Let me help with the rest of the jazz.

JEAN

There's not much more, Dan said to travel light. Dumped on you?

CYNTHIA

(*As they go out to the car*)
On us. Auggie's sister.
(KIRSTEN *follows them.*)

AUGUST

The place looks like a resort. You've never seen so many tourists in your life.

CHAD

(*Going out to the car.*)
I told him.

AUGUST

It gets worse every year. The girls? No, the girls are fine. They pitched their tents, made a cooking pit. Every goddamned one of them is an eagle scout.

DAN

(*He disappears for a moment, taking folders into* AUGUST'*s office.*)
Or whatever.

AUGUST

They're happy as bugs. Ask about you and Jean every ten minutes.

DAN

Don't say anything about Jean being pregnant; she doesn't want them pestering her.

AUGUST

I doubt I'll see them till September. My sister is dying again; she was scraped up off the street in Cleveland; apparently the hospitals there haven't the facilities or the will. How the hell they found us here—the man came to install the telephone, ten minutes later it was ringing.

DAN

She's dying?

AUGUST

Of course not, and she claims poverty so— Well, it's not worth talking about.

DAN

I've never met the lady.

AUGUST

I'm afraid there's no way I can protect you from it now.

CHAD

(*Re-entering with equipment, etc.*)

I had the windows opened forever. It's been a sopping spring; thought it wasn't gonna be any good for you guys, but it's cleared up some the last week.

DAN

Thank God.

AUGUST

Conditions are excellent. (JEAN, CYNTHIA, *and* KIRSTEN *re-enter with suitcases and knapsacks.*) We've got the bulldozer lined up for day after tomorrow; you might even be ready for it.

DAN
Oh, hell, let me help.

JEAN
That's it.

AUGUST
Jean, I'm really sorry about this.

JEAN
What's wrong with her?

AUGUST
(*Speaking in* CHAD'*s presence as one might speak before a waiter.*)
. . . I wouldn't know.

CYNTHIA
Acute "I wouldn't know," chronic "I suspect."

AUGUST
The hospital is flying her down tomorrow, unconscious and incognito.

CYNTHIA
And collect. (*To* JEAN) You and Dan are upstairs.

KIRSTEN
You're going to hate it. It's worse than last year.

CYNTHIA
Help carry that up and please don't be impossible.

KIRSTEN
(*Going.*)
If I was you, I'd have sent me to camp.

(CYNTHIA *follows her up.*)

CHAD
You visiting again, Doctor, or you planning to stay awhile?

JEAN
No, I'm booked for the duration.

CHAD
We'll have to get her out with us.

JEAN
Don't tell me Blue Shoals swings.

DAN
Out fishing, out to the lake.
(*He takes what he can carry of the baggage upstairs.*)

JEAN
No way. What happens when the lake comes in? Will you move the house?

CHAD
Electric company charge you eight hundred bucks for every line you cut . . . probably cost six, seven thousand to move it up the hill.

JEAN
You couldn't build it for that.

CHAD
Nobody'd want to either. Beams probably rotten, you couldn't get a block under it.

JEAN
(*As she goes upstairs, followed by Cynthia*)
Is it haunted?

CYNTHIA
Not that we've noticed.

CHAD
(*Going upstairs.*)
What do you want? You want it haunted or you want it
unhaunted? I'll go either way.

AUGUST
(*Slide: townspeople.*)
Townspeople who awaited with bated breath our discovery
of King Tut's tomb. (*Slide: students.*) Alleged students.
We were assisted last summer by eight girls and one pre-
sumed male from Dr. Loggins's class in field archaeology.
(*Slide:* CYNTHIA.) Ex-relation by marriage. (*Slide: camp-
site.*) This is the campsite of the students, pitched well
out of earshot of the house. (*Slide:* CYNTHIA.) Ex-relation.
(*Slide:* KIRSTEN.) Alleged daughter. (*Slide: picnic.*) Pic-
nic. (*Slide: people playing.*) Horse play. (*Slide: bathers.*)
Horse play at the lake. (*Slide:* CYNTHIA.) Horse.

DAN
(*As he comes back downstairs, followed by* JEAN *and*
CYNTHIA)
Come down to the site, you've got time.

AUGUST
I've got to talk money with some St. Louis real-estate men
this evening. This isn't going to be much of a vacation for
you, Jean.

DAN
(*Leaving.*)
Sure it will.

JEAN
Sure it will.

CYNTHIA
(*Opening refrigerator.*)
Sure it will. How about a drink?
(*She slams the door, effecting a blackout, except for a flashlight beam that investigates the deserted room.*)

DAN'S VOICE
Is someone there? Hello? (*Flashlight out.*) Hello? (*Sound of a stumble. Mumbled*) Oh, damnit. (*The flashlight comes on.* DAN *in pajamas gets up, goes to the lamp, turns it on.*)

CYNTHIA
(*Entering from the door, opening a carton of cigarettes.*)
Good Lord, I thought you'd be asleep hours ago.

DAN
I was, heard the weirdest . . .

CYNTHIA
Probably the kids on the dig.

DAN
Thought we were being burglarized.

CYNTHIA
Not much worry about that.

DAN
Are you just getting in? It must be two in the morning.

CYNTHIA
Cigarettes. You working tomorrow?

DAN
Oh, yeah, I'll be up and—

CYNTHIA
(*Cutting him off. Reaching for the lamp switch.*)
Better get to bed then.

(BLACKOUT.)

KIRSTEN'S VOICE
Mother. Mother. Mommy?

AUGUST'S VOICE
They won't hurt you. You were dreaming.

KIRSTEN'S VOICE
They were talking.

AUGUST'S VOICE
They're only shadows.

KIRSTEN'S VOICE
They were talking.

AUGUST'S VOICE
Shhhh.

KIRSTEN'S VOICE
They were talking.

(*Sundown the next evening.* CHAD *opens the front door as*
CYNTHIA *and* KIRSTEN *come downstairs.*)

CHAD
Got a delivery for you.

(AUGUST *enters, carrying* DELIA.)

AUGUST
Please don't squirm. I'm not that strong and you're not as dissipated as you'd like to believe.

DELIA
There is no point in dragging me inside. I'm not staying—

AUGUST
If you want to fight, wait till I set you down!

CYNTHIA
Just here on the—

DELIA
I'll go to a state hospital.

AUGUST
(*Panting.*)
No state has that kind of money.
(*He carries* DELIA *to a lounge.*)

DELIA
I'm not going to die in this godforsaken Grant Wood mausoleum.

AUGUST
(*Beat.*)
Good.

DELIA
How the hell did they find you?

AUGUST
I was wondering.

DELIA
You're making quite a name for yourself. That must be gratifying after all these—

AUGUST
—I've always been satisfied to leave the limelight to those—

DELIA
—That's the God's truth.

AUGUST
—to those who required it.

DELIA
(*Beat.*)
Yes, well, just as well.

AUGUST
Why were you in Cleveland?

DELIA
I don't know. It was important to go to— I met someone
from Cleveland, or I don't know. I was in Casablanca.
Detroit with palm trees! Vile people! Vile air! Vile cli-
mate! I went to Annaba, I went to Benghazi, I met someone from Portugal, I started to go back to Lisbon, I
changed my mind and went to—
(*Interrupted by a violent coughing spell.*)

AUGUST
(*Stands unmoved, watching her. Finally, as she relaxes*)
Where.

DELIA
(*After relaxing. Calmly*)
Cleveland. (*Pause.*) How long did they keep me? They
kept me a month, didn't they? Why?

DAN
(*Off, calling*)
Jean?

DELIA

I don't mean that; I'm not that bad.

JEAN
(*From upstairs*)
I'm up, I'll be down.

AUGUST
(*Taking medicine and papers from* CHAD.)
I've got instructions, yet. You were glad enough to get
away.

DELIA

They were trying to kill me in that goddamned hospital.
(*Jean comes down*)

AUGUST

They were not trying to kill—

DELIA

Whether they were killing
me through malice and in-
tention or killing me
through ignorance of medicine is immaterial. It
amounts to the same tor-
ture.

DAN
(*Entering, dirty and mildly
refractory.*)
What a day. Hi. Be glad
you didn't come down.

JEAN
Cynthia said.

AUGUST
(*Handing the paper to
her.*)
Jean, can you make any
sense of that?

CHAD

You're going to have a lot of fun with her.

KIRSTEN
For your information, she isn't well.

CYNTHIA
We can do very well without that.

AUGUST
Thank you very much, Mr. Jasker.

CHAD
Yeah, I'll see you around.

AUGUST
Jean, I don't think you and Dan have had the pleasure of meeting my sister. Dan and Jean Loggins, D. K. Eriksen.

DAN
I talked to you on the phone once.

AUGUST
Dan's my assistant. Jean's an intern gynecologist. If you're interested in discussing medicine, I'm sure she'll listen to you.

DELIA
"D.K." Call me Delia, that's the name Dad gave me.

JEAN
I've read your books, of course.

DELIA
That was another life, Doctor.

JEAN
If you're going to call me doctor, I'll have to call you Miss Eriksen.

DELIA
You know me. I don't *meet people*.

AUGUST
You're not to be moved.

DELIA
You know quite well this is just the sort of cozily scientific, cenobitic community that'll drive me bananas.

DAN
Oh, fine. Scientific. You should see it down there. It's a mob scene.

DELIA
No, thank you.

CYNTHIA
(*Getting a glass of wine.*)
Anyone else?

DAN
I'm trying to direct some jerk with a bulldozer . . .

CYNTHIA
That was worth seeing.

JEAN
I saw the cars from the house.

DAN
All day long it's been a cavalcade pouring into the field. Every family from the Mississippi to the Wabash. They got their kids, they got their picnic lunches, it looks like a fucking fairground. Where you been, people? I mean, we been here twenty-four hours already. You missed Professor Howe pulling up a patch of ragweed.

CYNTHIA
I enjoy the people showing up.

DAN
Oh, sure. "What's that thing?" Well, ma'am, that *thing* is
a surveyor's alidade. It sits on a tripod and you look
through here and see a family from Carbondale eating
fried chicken.

CYNTHIA
They go away when they find out August isn't going to let
them volunteer.

DAN
A girl says, "Why did they build those mounds?" What
mounds? Oh, the one over there. That they're using for a
parking lot. Well, honey, we excavated that mound last
summer and we found they had built that mound over
ninty-three Paducah High School cheerleaders.
(*Begins to roll a joint.*)

JEAN
He loves it, of course; he performs for them like a dancing
bear. The girls line up for his classes. They eat him up. I
don't know if they learn anything.

AUGUST
Any number of things, I'd think.

CYNTHIA
After August explains what we hope to find, the crowd
gets so bored they leave him talking to himself.

JEAN
(*Re: the medication*)
This is morning and evening—this is four times a day.

DAN

"Why did they build the mounds?"! They built the mounds for the same reason I'd build the mounds. Because I wanted to make myself conspicuous; to sacrifice to the gods; to protect me from floods, or animals; because my grandfather built mounds; because I was sick of digging holes; because I didn't have the technology to build pyramids and a person isn't happy unless he's building something.

CYNTHIA

There are people who'd be perfectly happy tearing something down.

DAN

A person isn't happy unless he's building something. Scratch a fry cook, you'll find an architect. Listen to Chad Jasker tell you about the restaurant he's going to build. I mean, he knows the kind of light fixtures he's going to have. Every society reaches the point where they build mounds. As the society becomes more sophisticated, the rationalization for building them becomes more sophisticated. For an accomplishment, honey, to bring me closer to Elysium; to leave something behind me for my grandchildren to marvel at. To say I'd built something!

AUGUST

I.e., if we find out, we'll let you know.

DELIA

Jesus, dear God, but it's bleak here. Bleak, bleak, bleak, bleak . . . Bleak farmland on a bleak pond by a bleak— I can't stay here, I—

AUGUST
Normally I might try to excuse her egocentric excen—

DELIA
(*Riding over*)
But my exploits are so notorious it's useless to closet my
presence here and we are forced to admit that I am con-
valescing from a riding accident . . . I fell from my horse.

AUGUST
It's rather more serious than it might sound, as it was a
flying horse.
(*He is pouring medicine for her.*)

DELIA
Jean, what is he giving me? I can't breathe. They gave him
something to give me, it's preventing me from—

AUGUST
The only drugs in your system are residual from your
binges in Benghazi and—wherever.

DELIA
I can't get air.

JEAN
You're breathing perfectly normally; if you weren't getting air, you'd be turning purple, or—

DELIA
—What the hell does a gynecologist know about cirrhosis
of the liver?

JEAN
Absolutely nothing; except that it doesn't occur in the
respiratory system.

DELIA

All right, I'm a hypochondriac, Jean. Ignore all requests for medical advice.

JEAN

Delia, after one week in the clinic, I could spot a hypochondriac at forty feet.

DAN

(*Who has been rolling a joint; passing it to* CYNTHIA, *who takes it, and* JEAN, *who passes it back.*)
She's not on call this summer, Delia, she's taking off eighteen months to have a baby.

JEAN

After that I might have a better idea of what I've been talking about.

DELIA

It doesn't take eighteen months to have a baby. It takes eighteen months to have a rhinoceros.

DAN

(*Regarding the joint. To* JEAN)
Take it.

JEAN

No, I said.

DAN

It's not tobacco, it won't kill you.

JEAN

Not now, thank you.

DAN

Only girl I've ever met who's a bigger drughead than I am, she gets pregnant and goes cold turkey on me.

JEAN
Don't mention the offspring to the girls, we don't want it generally—

DELIA
I will not be cross-examined by a mob of swaddling adolescents.

CYNTHIA
Never fear; they aren't allowed near the place.

JEAN
I thought they might.

CYNTHIA
—That's verboten. No students, no dogs.

DAN
I mean, I can understand giving up alcohol and meat. Well, meat, but an innocent joint.

JEAN
(From "giving up")
Oh, come on, really—I don't know why it should bother you; I'm the one who's straight.

CYNTHIA
You can't give up meat. You need all the protein you can get.

JEAN
(Overlapping)
No, I'm eating perfectly normally; I'm just trying to avoid toxins. And you don't require nearly the amount of protein you're led to believe. We just thought we'd give it every opportunity to make its own problems.

CYNTHIA
Don't think it won't.

DAN
I can imagine the little bugger deprived of—

JEAN
O.K., so it will. That's a person's prerogative; we'll try to
help, and undoubtedly screw up completely. Good God,
it's lousy grass anyway.

DAN
O.K., O.K., go to bed.

JEAN
(*Leaving.*)
I am, thank you.

DELIA
(*Overlapping*)
Get me out of this thing. I'm going to be sick.

DAN
Where's she staying?

KIRSTEN
Up in my room with me.

DELIA
Oh, dear God—

DAN
I'll take you. (*Picking her up and carrying her off.*) If
you bite me or throw up, I'll drop you right on the floor.

(KIRSTEN *follows them off. Beat.*)

CYNTHIA
Is she all right?

AUGUST
She's fine.

CYNTHIA
I realize she's down and out; she's undoubtedly broke.

AUGUST
I don't think so.

CYNTHIA
And although she's not bothered to contact us more than
three times in ten years, you could feel that we've neglected her—

AUGUST
Not as much as she's neglected herself.

CYNTHIA
Or been neglected by her reading public.

AUGUST
I doubt she ever had much of a reading public.

CYNTHIA
August, it is a challenge enough to maintain civilization
on these summer-long bivouacs without nursing—

AUGUST
Ignore her; Dad did. Laugh at her.

CYNTHIA
She isn't funny. Could you at least get someone out here
to look after her so—

AUGUST
We can't begin to afford it.

CYNTHIA
One of the girls could help—

AUGUST
Their parents are paying a thousand dollars a head for a
credit in field archaeology, not for a nursing—

CYNTHIA
They're paying to get them out of the house.

AUGUST
Jean is a practicing intern at—

CYNTHIA
—You can't expect Jean to take up residence as the—

AUGUST
Ignore her, damnit, you have enough to do. Ignore her.
She doesn't like you anyway.

DAN
(*In from upstairs, out the door.*)
I'm going to take a walk. The girls said someone was
snooping around the dig last night. We haven't even
started, we've got prowlers; I don't know what they think
we're going to find. What do they think we're going to
find?

CYNTHIA
(*Going upstairs.*)
She likes me fine, August. She always has. It's you she can't
stand.

AUGUST
(*Alone.*)
Well, fine, fine, fine, good, good. (*As the slides change
furiously*) Dianne, this wreckage appears to be in a state
of organization you will undoubtedly recognize as typical
of my wife. Please throw away those works of her genius

which do not pertain to the excavation. Mrs. Howe, with
stunning evidence to the contrary, persists in believing
she is Diane Arbus. My sister, for instance, is of marginal
archaeological interest. (*Slide: site.*) This is the rather
unprepossessing site as we found it. The trial pit—stratig-
raphy exposed seven separate layers of occupation on the
site. (*Site.*) A bulldozer was employed to remove a dense
growth of weeds and about four inches of root-bearing top-
soil. The remaining four to six inches of humus above the
plow sole was cleared by hand and screened. (*Slide: projectile points.*) This soil proved to be the repository of Late
Woodland artifacts of surpassing mediocrity which were
joyfully displayed to me chip by chip. (*Six quick slides of
the lake.*) This is the lake. (*As* JEAN *comes down, dawn
arrives and* CHAD *enters.*) This is the lake. This is the lake.
This is the lake. This is the lake. This is the—
(CHAD *framed against the lake.*)

CHAD
(*Immediately, as* AUGUST *stands in stunned remembrance*)
Last summer I didn't really figure you to marry Dan. You
seemed to be pretty sure of what you wanted.

JEAN
Dan and I wanted more or less the same thing, I think.

CHAD
I tell you what, I got the car out front; there's something
I want to show you.

JEAN
I don't think so.

CHAD
—You don't even know what it is.

JEAN
—I know, but nevertheless—

CHAD
—You only live once.

JEAN
I'm not sure that's been proved.

CHAD
The courthouse. What can happen? Who's gonna miss you?

JEAN
I've seen it.

CHAD
Inside?

JEAN
No, I haven't been inside.

CHAD
—See, now, you don't know. I want to show you.

JEAN
What?

CHAD
Will you come?

JEAN
No. I can't, Chad; what?

CHAD
You'll promise to see it?

JEAN
When I go into town again.

CHAD

There's a model of damn near the whole county laid out
—it's huge—guess what it's called. The whole model—

JEAN

I can't guess, I really don't think—

CHAD

(*Overlapping*)
—O.K., O.K., I'm not playing with you—you promised.
It's called Jasker's Development. The Jasker Development. They got . . . the hills, they got all the buildings,
the mounds are on it—the ones that are left—they even got
little trees set up—and this big, beautiful blue lake—like—
not round, but maple-shaped, hand-shaped. We been talking six years to get Washington to give it to us.

JEAN

The mounds that are left?

CHAD

Four of them will be left, the other five the Interstate will
take out. It's all part and parcel with the development.
The lake and the new Interstate. See, we got 57 from
Chicago already, which they're widening, and the new
Interstate cuts across us the other way with all these inter-
changes and all. It all goes—aw, hell, it'll just take fifteen
minutes to see the damn model and understand what's
happening—

JEAN

—No, I'm sure. You can feel it. We're an anachronism.
Squint your eyes and you can already see girls water-skiing
over the tops of the hawthorn trees. Restaurants with

dance bands. It's all changing. The lake has become the fact, hasn't it?

CHAD

Pretty much.

JEAN

And you'll own a lot of the shoreline, won't you?

CHAD

Good piece. I could show you if we—

JEAN

—Come on, really—

CHAD

—Well, it's not how much we own, it's where it is. See— Dad was smart enough not to sell. Only thing he ever did— Guys were coming down from Memphis—See, we're sitting on the lake and the interchange.

JEAN

So you're right in the middle of it.

CHAD

We *are* the middle of it—we didn't even know. You wouldn't recognize this town if you'd seen it five years ago. Like, it didn't start being a tourist attraction till a few years ago; but all of a sudden Lily-Tulip is buying up twenty acres to build a new home office, a national head-quarters with landscaping, and another one—a box com-pany—cardboard boxes, and everybody's trying to buy our place. These guys from Memphis are talking to brok-ers and the brokers are driving out to chew it over with us, you know. And their offer goes up and it goes up, Dad just sits tight on it—and finally these guys come down to talk to us themselves, and they say, all right, you're not going to sell—you got the place we want to build on—what would you say about giving us a *lease*.

JEAN
Oh . . . that could mean a lot more.

CHAD
Every month, month on month for as long as they're in operation. They been working over a year. Memphis is the main office of the Holiday Inn people. They've got their market studies, their books full of figures, they've got their artists'-concepts drawings already. They got their 800-unit motel, they got their swimming pools, and the facilities to the lake, they got a layout would amaze . . . (*Floating*) . . . Dream of something. Dream of something you want . . . anything. A restaurant with twenty-four-hour service—dream of anything you want. They showed us rug samples that thick—with padding under it. See, we're sitting on the lake and the interchange.

JEAN
All first-class stuff.

CHAD
A barber sh—ah, beauty parlor. A uh—the clubs, the little —with clubs . . .

JEAN
Sauna?

CHAD
No, you hit the damn ball, the little setup for a—

JEAN
Tennis court?

CHAD

Tennis court, too, but those—oh, shit. Golf! Little golf—

JEAN

Miniature golf.

CHAD

No, that's kids, that's toys— Chip and putt! Chip and putt. For practicing.

JEAN

Never heard of it.

CHAD

It's like where you learn, you practice—*you* never heard of it! *I* never had a golf club in my *hand!* There's a golf course at Marion, eighty miles off, probably the closest place you could go— I probably couldn't hit— (*Enjoying himself, nearly laughing*) —I'd dig up the green; they'd kick me off the—but I'm going to! Hell! Go out chipping and putting; get me a pair of the shorts and the socks and the cap and those gloves they wear— Chip and putt with the pros, man. Lee Trevino's.

JEAN

You'll be terrific.

CHAD

You know what we get? Three percent. On every dollar spent.

JEAN

That's amazing; that's a lot.

CHAD

Of everything except food. One percent on food and drink . . . that's the deal they're offering us.

JEAN

You will be rich. That's what I find so profound about politics; the grace notes of that kind of power. The signing of an energy bill in Washington transforms rural areas into resorts—field hands into busboys.

CHAD

Yeah.

JEAN

They shall beat their plowshares into Pontiacs.

CHAD

(*Almost holding his breath*)

. . . I . . . got six acres all my own. For a house. On an island. I got an island—it will be. Out a little bit on the lake. Looks right across to it. Be able to sit on the lawn and watch people drive up off there to the motel—say that's another ten bucks. That guy over there's havin' himself a beer, that's two cents!—

(*A long pause; as she starts to move.*)

JEAN

You'll get a kick out of it.

CHAD

Hey . . . (*She stops.*) I'll give it to you . . . Anything you want, it's yours. I'll sign it over. You're the only thing I ever saw I really wanted.

JEAN

(*Long pause.*)

No.

CHAD

I want you to—

JEAN
—Chad—get lost.

(CYNTHIA *enters with* KIRSTEN.)

CHAD
Thought I'd come over and see if you people got rained
on last night.

CYNTHIA
Did we? You didn't say anything about it.

JEAN
No.

CYNTHIA
Of course no one's out at the dig till it dries up this afternoon; we're all holed up here.

(JEAN *leaves,* KIRSTEN *follows her.*)

CHAD
I'm gonna need some bread. About thirty dollars.

CYNTHIA
(*Beat.*)
So you can have another night with the locals on rye-and-
ginger?

CHAD
Come on, I got some buddies waiting for me in town.

(CYNTHIA *reaches for her purse as they exit.*)

AUGUST
(*Alone—no slide.*)
Note to myself. Separate personal from professional. Dis-
card personal. Separate separate from separate; separate

personal from imaginary, illusion from family, ancient
from contemporary, etc., if possible. Organize if possible
and separate if possible from if impossible. Catalogue what
shards remain from the dig; celebrate separation; also, organize (a) brain, (b) photographic material, (c) letter of
resignation, (d) health, (e) budget, (f) family, (f-1)
family—ties, (g) life. Not necessarily in that order. Dianne,
if you're still with me, copy that out and don't worry
about it.

(Slide of a pot. DELIA *is on the lounge;* JEAN *is repeatedly
doing a sit-up exercise during the following scene.* KIRSTEN
sits watching DELIA.)

AUGUST
This is a shell-tempered pot that we found four years ago
in one of the mounds. What the hell it's doing in here only
God and the photographer could tell you.

CYNTHIA
(Entering past AUGUST.)
My eyes are driving me crazy. I don't think the muscles
have the strength to focus on anything more this morning.

JEAN
Spots?

CYNTHIA
(Falling back into a chair.)
Worse: one spot. I've been batting at a nonexistent fly all
day. Everyone at the site waved at me.

JEAN
I might wander down and see how they're doing later.

CYNTHIA

They'll be up. Don't go today, it's too slow. They're digging out post molds. It takes forever and they're not uncovering anything but dark spots. (*To* DELIA) I hope you weren't cold last night; it can get pretty nippy in June, we—

DELIA

I froze.

CYNTHIA

What?

DELIA

I froze.

CYNTHIA

(*Getting up again.*)
I'll get the blankets from our room. We all practically sleep outside from March to November.

DELIA

(*Overlapping from* CYNTHIA'*s "all"*)
I'm fine now. I'm fine now.

CYNTHIA

Do you have clothes or anything that we should send for? Other than what's in the trunk?

DELIA

What trunk?

CYNTHIA

The trunk you shipped from Oran.

DELIA

Did I? Good.

CYNTHIA

The hospital discovered your identity by redeeming the claim check on your trunk.

DELIA

That's—resourceful of them.

CYNTHIA

Do you have anything that—

DELIA

Don't worry about it.

CYNTHIA

We're so schizophrenic since we've been coming down here. Just as I begin adjusting to a life stripped down to what I can carry on my back we—

JEAN

—pull up camp—

CYNTHIA

—migrate back to eleven rooms of memorabilia.

JEAN

I don't think Delia's a collector.

DELIA

I collect with one hand and mislay with the other. The world's unclaimed-baggage departments are crammed with my paraphernalia.

CYNTHIA

I know it's going to sound fatuously supportive, but you're looking better. How are you feeling?

DELIA

Better.

JEAN
Don't rub your eyes.

CYNTHIA
Oh, I know . . .

DELIA
Don't stare at the Gorgon, Kirsten; you'll turn to stone.

CYNTHIA
You have a fan.

KIRSTEN
Where's Oran?

DELIA
Tunisia—Algeria.

JEAN
That sounds very glamorous to us landlubbers.

DELIA
It isn't. Oran was Camus's model for the *locus in quo* of *The Plague*. We were host to every fly on the Mediterranean.

KIRSTEN
Were you there with your husband?

CYNTHIA
Kirsten, she isn't married any more, you know that.

DELIA
(*Simultaneously*)
Good God, I haven't been married since before you were born. I don't even remember being married. I can't believe—
(*Trailing into laugh.*)

KIRSTEN
You remember being—

DELIA
—I was very young, darling; I was terrified of rejection; what I remember is an anxiety to please so severe I could hardly fight down the panic long enough to get drunk. I was bonded, I wasn't—
(*Coughs.*)

KIRSTEN
You don't remember what he looked like?

CYNTHIA
Honey, don't bother her.

DELIA
No, it's fine—He was a strong, hirsute, sweating, horny cocksman. He sold drilling equipment. I was so captivated that that didn't strike me as funny until years after I got out from under him.

KIRSTEN
I thought he was an artist.

DELIA
God, no, God, no—God no! He has not eyes in his head! We traveled through the East. He traveled, I trailed.

JEAN
You were working, though.

DELIA
Self-defense.

KIRSTEN
New England or the Far East?

DELIA

Egypt, Lebanon, Syria, Cyprus, Metaxa, Ouzo, Grappa, Cinzano . . .

AUGUST

(*Off*)

. . . as long as it's considered subservient to anthropology. We'll never have sufficient clout till we have a separate autonomous department.

DAN

(*As he and* AUGUST *enter*)

Man, it's hotter than a pistol out there.

(AUGUST *goes to his office,* DAN *to the refrigerator.*)

CYNTHIA

Tell me about it.

KIRSTEN

And you split.

CYNTHIA

Don't bother her, Kirsten—

DELIA

And I split. But once set in motion, the moving object tends to remain in motion.

CYNTHIA

Well, maybe the stationary object now will tend to remain stationary.

DELIA

Couldn't do that. Couldn't do that. I have a very real terror of gathering moss.

(DAN *opens a beer.*)

CYNTHIA
I don't know how you stay thin—

JEAN
It'll catch up with him.

DAN
(*To* DELIA)
I think I might welcome a little moss after your experiences.

DELIA
After how many years? Eight, nine—

JEAN
Don't, I'm counting—

DELIA
—After living in the liquid world, wouldn't I welcome being washed up onto some sandy lakeshore-front property in the sun to dry out. Out in the thin air where the hand is quicker than the eye and noises are distinct and occur at their source rather than inside your head. Well, I'm— vaguely conscious of allowing myself to float up toward the surface—at least to look around.

CYNTHIA
Good.

DELIA
Whereupon I'm certain I'll want to drown myself.

DAN
Again.

JEAN
(*Giving up the exercises.*)
Oh. Uncle. A hundred ten.

44 THE MOUND BUILDERS

44   THE MOUND BUILDERS

KIRSTEN
Up toward the surface to look around.

DELIA
Hello. Good morning. What's for breakfast? I hope you weren't cold last night.

JEAN
Is that O.K.?

DAN
(*Looking through typed pages.*)
All that only typed up to four pages?

JEAN
How are the post molds coming?

DAN
"Post molds"? You've been reading books.

JEAN
Talking to Cynthia.

DAN
(*To* CYNTHIA)
We're ready on the third section while the girls are taking a lunch break if you want to get at it.

CYNTHIA
They can wait.

JEAN
What were the posts for?

CYNTHIA
Walls. You've never seen so many holes in your life.

DAN

These are for the walls of a roundhouse. They set posts
around in a circle about every two feet then filled in the
walls with mud and dabble. Walls about yea thick—fire pit
in the middle—no chimney, only one door—must have
been smoky as hell. Men only—sat around telling hunting
stories.

CYNTHIA

Then there must be about forty houses.

DAN

We won't get to them all, just a general configuration.

JEAN

This isn't really a typical village, is it?

DAN

Oh, yeah, pretty much.

CYNTHIA

Boringly so.

JEAN

In your notes you say that the typical village configuration
is a large plaza with a mound at each end—

DAN

The downtown area. A mound for the high muck-a-muck
God-King, and a mound for the temple.

JEAN

—and a street running around the plaza with houses all
around the four sides of the plaza, all very geometrically
laid out.

DAN

Very good. Roundhouse we're working on is down here in the corner.

JEAN

Swell. Only where are the mounds in the middle of the plaza?

KIRSTEN

Jasker plowed them under.

DAN

They were plowed under. That's why we didn't know there was a village here.

JEAN

And they weren't burial mounds so who would know—

DAN

No, burial mounds aren't associated with a village. They're a lot earlier. Burial mounds were built by hunters and gatherers; they didn't have a permanent village. There weren't any villages to speak of until the Mississippian Culture moved into the area and began to develop agriculture.

CYNTHIA

Then they had to hang around the house and tend the fields—sacrifice to the gods of harvest and whatnot.

DAN

There's been at least three different cultures who built mounds in the area—the Adena, back around 600 B.C.

JEAN
B.C.? 600 B.C.?

CYNTHIA
Don't ask; you don't want to know.

DAN
600 B.C. Then the Hopewell Culture. They both built burial mounds. Then along about A.D. 700 a whole new people moved into the area, and instead of building burial mounds, they built a mound and on top of the mound built a temple. Two mounds. One for their temple and one for their God-King.

JEAN
One at each end of the plaza.

DAN
And we call these people the Temple Mound People. Or for short, the Early Mississippian Culture.

JEAN
And those are our guys.

CYNTHIA
All very filled with pomp and circumstance.

JEAN
Cahokia, up in St. Louis, was one of the Mississippian cities, wasn't it?

DAN
Yeah. Probably forty, fifty thousand. Bigger than Paris or London at the time.

JEAN
I know, I was reading your book on it.

DAN
I knew it; let me tell you, don't read books.

JEAN

Do you get the feeling that they were just the least bit
weird?

CYNTHIA

Oh, definitely.

JEAN

There's a grave with six men all laid out ceremonially,
with their right hands chopped off.

CYNTHIA

You find that all the time.

JEAN

Well, I mean, really. Do they have an explanation for that?

CYNTHIA

Maybe they were caught masturbating. (*Beat.*) Where's
your book on circulation? I haven't seen you crack a
medical book since you've been here.

JEAN

What's more immediate is a stack of articles I've intended
to read for three months.

CYNTHIA

Well, don't hire out as a typist. August spends all his time
drumming up money to hire secretaries to type up Dan's
notes.

JEAN

You don't know how ignorant I am about the—

CYNTHIA

Well, stay that way. I'm not joking. Don't start. (*To* DAN)
Have one of the girls do it. (*To* JEAN) It's a full-time job
and you already have one.

JEAN
Two.

DAN
(*Unfazed by anything.*)
I'd do it myself but I can't type and I can't spell.

JEAN
What will you do after the Interstate levels the mounds
you're supposed to dig next summer?

AUGUST
(*Off, calling*)
—Dan? Where'd you put it?

DAN
(*Laying down pages.*)
Where'd I put what?

CYNTHIA
Really, don't bother with it.

DAN
(*Giving* JEAN *a pat in passing.*)
That's terrific. Come down later.

JEAN
Oh, God. I don't mind correcting your spelling, but please
don't pat me on the head.

DAN
(*Laughing, going into the office.*)
Where'd I put what?
(*He shuts the door behind him.*)

CYNTHIA
Have you learned anything about pregnancy that's going
to revolutionize childbirth?

JEAN

Oh . . . no. The source of that smug glow pregnant
women have. You really do feel the miracle of it all. Every
woman is the only woman who's ever been pregnant. That
—and one moment of blinding damnation that was probably singular to me. After two immediate miscarriages and
all kinds of anxiety about it—

CYNTHIA

I didn't realize you'd—

JEAN

Well, as grandmother would say, "Our women have a history of it"— That's why I'm reluctant to accept premature
congratulations. Still, when I finally managed to stay pregnant for two months and told Dan that maybe we were
O.K.—I felt for one second that in telling him I had
breached a covenant between me and the baby. As though
I had—forever fallen from grace. Did you feel that?

CYNTHIA

Fallen from grace, I wouldn't remember; the miracle, yes.

AUGUST

(*Re-entering with* DAN.)
But that has nothing to do with us.

DAN

Just tell them we've thought of calling the dig the First
National Bank of Carbondale Village.

AUGUST

That would do it. Kirsten's coming along and trying to
look deprived.

KIRSTEN

I think we do better when I look hopeful.

DAN
(*To* JEAN)
Come down and dig out a post mold with us.
(DELIA *laughs*.)

JEAN
It doesn't sound very romantic. It's more—what—rural
than the spectacular cultures, isn't it?

AUGUST
It was quite spectacular—take her up to the Koster Site.

JEAN
I mean like the Aztec Empire.

DAN
The Aztec culture was not really an empire.

JEAN
Well, or the Incan culture.

AUGUST
The Incans had an empire. We'd be working somewhere
else if our work here wasn't important.

DAN
If Cortes had landed here in 1250, you wouldn't be talking
about the Aztecs at all; you'd be talking about the glory
that was Jasker's Field. They had longer trade routes—
they just didn't leave anyone around to translate their
poetry.

JEAN
They had poetry?

AUGUST
I would imagine. Poetry, drama—the Aztecs did.

JEAN

Do we know any of it? The Aztec—

AUGUST

Yes, otherwise we—

JEAN

What did it sound like?

AUGUST

(*To* CYNTHIA)

I'll give you a ring about five.

(*He exits.*)

DAN

Free verse, rhyming verse; think Emily Dickinson:

Here are our precious flowers and songs
May our friends delight in them,
May the sadness fade out of our hearts.
This earth is only lent to us.
We shall have to leave our fine work.
We shall have to leave our beautiful flowers.
That is why I am sad as I sing for the sun.

DELIA

Who was that?

DAN

We don't know his name, Delia. We only know his work.

(*He exits.*)

CYNTHIA

(*Picking up her equipment as* JEAN *begins exercising.*)

Do you really think you'll go on with a medical career
after you have the baby?

JEAN
(*Stops dead. Beat.*)
It didn't stop you. You managed. Don't rub your—

CYNTHIA
I have several thousand photographs of Kirsten. Maybe
you'll go into pediatrics. (*Pause.*) If you come down,
bring a hat; the sun's murder.
(*Starts out.*)

JEAN
Were you into a photographic career before—

CYNTHIA
(*Overlapping*)
Not at all, not at all. I'm sorry I brought it up.
(JEAN *goes to the door as* CYNTHIA *leaves.*)

JEAN
(*After* CYNTHIA *has gone, looking after her.*)
Oh, brother.

DELIA
Did they fight? (JEAN *looks around to her.*) The Temple
Mound people?

JEAN
(*Not really thinking about it*)
Apparently. When they came—I think everyone would like
to agree that they were runaways from the Toltecs, but
haven't found substantial correlation; the books are all
very careful about sweeping pronouncements, but it's all
looking like a mud version of the Toltecs—so when they
came up they fought off whoever was here. And built the
first fortifications and all that. Probably kept the first
slaves.

DELIA
You feed it all into a computer—all the facts and fancies
the doctors have printed or typed or brushed and the computer would print out NOTHING APPLIES. It doesn't scan.
The truth is in dreams and nightmares, but you haven't
succeeded in getting that down. Rank was the ultimate
genius, sure, but he couldn't tell you how to keep from
cutting your wrist while you're shaving your legs.

JEAN
So you stopped shaving your legs.

DELIA
Cause and—
(*Coughs.*)

JEAN
(*Beat.*)
Effect. I wouldn't think you'd have much faith in com-
puters.

DELIA
Well—"faith" . . .

JEAN
Exactly.

DELIA
It's all going to be facts, Doctor. Art is part of a primitive
culture, really. The future is photography. We won't have
time for anything more subtle than lies.

JEAN
You have a way of conveying the impression you know all
the answers.

DELIA

The answer to which is, Yes, but I don't know any of the questions.

JEAN

Neat.

DELIA

Isn't that neat? It's a lie, but it's neat. I know the questions by rote. I just don't stand up well under them.

JEAN

No, neither do I. I won the spelling bee when I was a kid. Did beautifully, then had a complete collapse.

DELIA

I'd think so.

JEAN

Learned a lot of words.

DELIA

That's usually enough for a good impression. Spelling bee? God.

JEAN

The spelling bee. When I was what? Twelve. National Champion.

DELIA

Dear God.

JEAN

No one in the neighborhood went to the dictionary, they all came to me. I was tutored by my grandmother so I was the only kid who used the old-fashioned English grammar school method of syllable spelling. Charmed the pants off them. It started out as a kind of phenomenon or trick—then when my teachers realized they had a certifiable freak on their hands, they made me study for it.

DELIA

We're all freaks—all us bright sisters.

JEAN

It wasn't so bad until the competitions started. I mean, it wasn't like the little girl practicing her violin with her nose against the windowpane, watching all the other little girls at play. But I managed to work it into a nervous breakdown. (*Pause.*) I couldn't stop. Every word that was said to me, I spelled in my head. (*In an easy, flowing, but mechanical rhythm*) Mary, go to bed. Mary go to bed. Mary. M-A-R-Y. Mary. Go. G-O. Go. Mary go. To. T-O. To. Mary go to. Bed. B-E-D. Bed. Mary go to bed. Mary go to bed: M-A-R-Y-G-O-T-O-B-E-D. Mary, go to bed.

DELIA

Mary?

JEAN

Mary Jean. (*She wanders to the door to gaze out.*) That, and I lost the meaning. Mary, go to bed was syllables, not sense. (*Beat.*) Then there were days when the world and its objects separated, disintegrated into their cellular structure, molecular—worse—into their atomic structure. And nothing held its form. The air was the same as the trees and a table was no more substantial than the lady sitting at it . . . Those were . . . not good days.

DELIA

I don't imagine. But you got it together.

JEAN

Oh, yes. Juvenile resilience.

DELIA

And that led one directly into gynecology.

JEAN

That led one directly into an institution, and contact with
some very sick kids. Some of them more physically ill than
neurotic—who were not being particularly well cared for;
and that led to an interest in medicine. And reading your
books and others at an impressionable age led to gynecology. (*Beat.*) Also, living with my grandmother and her
cronies, who were preoccupied with illness, kept it pretty
much in my curiosity. They were always talking about
friends with female troubles, problems with their organs.
Of course, the only organ I knew was at church. I devel-
oped a theory of musical instruments as families. The cello
was the mother, the bass was the father, and all the violins
were the children. And the reason the big father organ at
Grace Methodist Church made such a mournful sound was
that female organs were always having something wrong
with them.

DELIA

Round John Virgin.

JEAN

Exactly.

DELIA

Have you seen Dad's book on the eye? Vision, actually?

JEAN

I didn't know he had one. He was a doctor?

DELIA

Physiologist. Hated practicing physicians. Eye, ear, nose, throat.

JEAN

Somewhat different field.

DELIA

I'd guess. The downstairs of the house was his, his consultation room, his office, his examination rooms: big square masculine Victorian rooms with oversized charts of the musculature of the neck and diagrams of the eye with the retina and rods and cones and iris and lens and those lines projected out into space indicating sight. And it appeared to me—still does—that rather than the eye being a muscle that collects light, those beams indicated that the eye projects vision onto the outside.
(*Pause.*)

JEAN

The place has changed since last year. I came down a couple of times last summer—weekends—watching their progress. But something odd is happening now—or not happening. There's something . . . I don't think it's the pregnancy, I think it's *here*. Or maybe my eyes are just projecting vision onto the outside.

DELIA

No, I don't think that's quite it.

JEAN

I have an intense desire to turn to the end of the chapter and see how it all comes out. You don't happen to have a deck of tarot on you, do you?

DELIA
No, I just look that way.

JEAN
It's only an anxiety.

DELIA
Generally speaking, Jean, ignore the Ides of March, but beware soothsayers. (JEAN *laughs*.) The old woman in *Dombey and Son* comes upon Edith in a lonely wood and says: "Give me a shilling and I'll tell your fortune." And Edith, of course, cuts her dead and goes on—Edith cuts everyone dead. And the old woman screams: "Give me a shilling or I'll yell your fortune after you."

JEAN
Oh, God. I'd pay. God, would I pay.

DELIA
That's what I thought.

JEAN
Jesus. Would I ever. What was the fortune? (*Pause*.) What was the—

DELIA
Give me a shilling or I'll tell you.

JEAN
Don't! Don't do that. What was the fortune?

DELIA
Uh, someone intervened.

JEAN
The hero.

DELIA
The villain actually.

JEAN
Do you do that? Turn to the end of a book to find out—

DELIA
No, I don't—I don't read any more.

JEAN
You do, of course. What's wrong is this inaction. I'm used to doing things. The university funds a clinic, you can't imagine. Coming off that is like coming off speed.

DELIA
And that's your answer. Why do you want to be a doctor when we get such a kick from diagnosing our own case? What seems to be the problem, Mrs. Blue—"Well, Doctor, I'm afraid I'm going to require twenty-five 300-milligram capsules of Declomycin."

JEAN
Oh, it's true. A gargle and forty Ornade spansules.

DELIA
Jean's only coming down off work and D.K. is frantically beating the bushes for something to believe in. Something with passion to warm up the blood and make her forget where it hurts. Great blinders is believing in and she's a great believer in blinders.

JEAN
Where does it hurt, D.K.?

DELIA
Doctor, it's a pain in the ass.

JEAN
Where does it hurt, D.K.?

DELIA
I thought we agreed not to ask.

(BLACKOUT—*slide utterly black with a hint of fire some-where.*)

AUGUST
I think this would be the tribal weenie roast.

CHAD'S VOICE
(*Drunk, pounding the door.*)
Goddamn! Cynthia?

CYNTHIA'S VOICE
(*Harsh whisper*)
What are you doing? The house is full of people, none of whom have ever been known to sleep!

CHAD'S VOICE
(*Drunk, urgent*)
I gotta go. I had to come over. I had to come.

CYNTHIA'S VOICE
Shhhhhh! Good God, are you drunk?

CHAD'S VOICE
I drunk thirty dollars' worth of rye-and-ginger since six o'clock.

CYNTHIA'S VOICE
Oh, God. Come outside.

CHAD'S VOICE
When you need it, we go. We gotta go when I need it, damnit.

CYNTHIA'S VOICE
Come outside; come on outside.

CHAD'S VOICE
(*Louder, insistent*)
I'm hot, baby—get down; take it, goddamnit; it'll just be ten seconds; nobody's gonna come in in ten seconds.

CYNTHIA'S VOICE
Shhhh. Come on.

CHAD'S VOICE
Come on.

CYNTHIA'S VOICE
Shh. Come on, come outside.

(*The screen-door spring sounds as they are heard to go outside. Flashlight.*)

DAN
Is someone there? Hello? (*Flashlight out.*) Hello? (*Stumbles.*) Oh, goddamnit. (*Flashlight on, he's on his knees, the light finds the lamp, he turns it on.* DELIA *is on the lounge, a hand averting the light from her eyes.*) Oh. Oh! Shit. Oh, baby. Oh, wow! I'm sorry. Oh, Jesus . . . I thought we were being burglarized . . . Oh, you scared the piss out of me.
(*He sits down.*)

DELIA
(*Still with her hand averting the light. Flatly*)
Any time.

DAN
Couldn't you have coughed or something? Were you asleep?

DELIA

No.

DAN

Wooooooow! You expect to see someone. Then you do see someone. Wow! You couldn't sleep?

DELIA

I don't know.

DAN

I'm a light sleeper.

DELIA

(*Only a glance at him.*)
Why don't you straighten up like a man? Your posture is a disgrace to the species.

DAN

That's probably from working in—

DELIA

—Oh, for godsake, put your shoulders down, you look like a capon. I'm not talking about your physical health. I'm talking about this Howdy-Dowdy, hale-fellow, nice-guy, innocent-babe-in-the-woods façade you splash over every — I'm a writer, I'm not a chiropractor.

DAN

You still think of yourself as a writer? (*She looks at him directly for the first time.*) I mean, I'm glad; are you working? Are you writing? You know, I knew August for two years before I knew you were his sister? We read you at school . . . Contemporary American Lit. Professor . . . can't remember. Read half your second book aloud. Second one was *Spindrift?* (*Pause.*) He was wild about it.

Read everything aloud because he knew (a) we wouldn't
read anything he assigned, and he had this thing that any
really good book should be read aloud (b) .
(*He begins rolling a joint.*)

DELIA

Sounds like a lousy disciplinarian.

DAN

Frustrated actor. Read terrifically.

DELIA

Snap course.

DAN

No shit; that's all I took my last year.

DELIA

Where was this?

DAN

Columbia. Said you were the last defender of a woman's
right to make a fool of herself.

DELIA

Oh, surely not the last. Tell him I was drunk.

DAN

When you wrote it? Does that make it bad?

DELIA

No. It makes it easier. No, it doesn't. Nothing makes it
easier—
(*Mumbles, a light cough.*)

DAN

What?

DELIA
(*Forced out*)
I said nothing makes it easier once it starts becoming diffi-
cult! Half of it. Half of it should read very nicely. Half of
it was dictated into a tape recorder. Because I couldn't find
the typewriter—keys.

DAN
I liked it.

DELIA
The half you heard.

DAN
I read it. I like it a lot. I realize you couldn't care less one
way or the other whether I—

DELIA
(*Overlapping almost from "realize"*)
I had a little secretary come in from some agency and type
it for me. Temporary help. She looked . . . "temporary."
Very neat, sweet, meek. She typed eight hours a day for five
days, never misspelling a word, stacked the manuscript on
the desk, put on her neat, sweet, meek gloves while I wrote
out a check; took her check sweetly, put on her coat
meekly, and left by the front door neatly. And I took the
manuscript, put it in a box, wrapped it in vinegar and
brown paper, addressed it to my publisher, who had been
expecting it daily for over five months, threw it on the
closet floor, and got drunk for three days. Wouldn't answer
the phone.

DAN
Because it was finished?

DELIA
Because I thought she hadn't liked it.

DAN
(*Pause.*)
And after three days?

DELIA
The police, with my publisher, broke the door in. I told him it was going to be a failure. Later on he told me the book was a success but I was a failure.

DAN
I liked it very much. (*Beat. He gets up, looking out again.*) Was that you? That clamor down here?

DELIA
You've been coming here four summers? You and Auggie and Cynthia? I'd think you'd have noticed that you're in the country out here. The natives get restless at night. The dogs raid the hen houses. They get hungry.

DAN
(*Offering the joint*)
Want a toke?

DELIA
How did you ever survive four years in New York?

DAN
Five, I got my M.S. (DELIA *laughs.*) It was really intimidating, but I kinda loved it. I had this great roommate who worried about me. Thought he was Seymour Glass. The guy in all the—

DELIA
I'm familiar—

DAN

Studied medieval history, but he was a nice guy—

DELIA

—Well, though, medieval history isn't something to cross off lightly, he could have told you how the Flemish used a virgin to distract the horny unicorn.

DAN

We used to put him on.

DELIA

Yes, I'm sure—

DAN

—Well, then, also, I really believed the only way to feel completely safe on the sidewalks of New York is to be completely, knockdown drunk. I mean visibly, stinking, reeling, dangerously drunk.

DELIA

How many times have you been dangerously—

DAN

On the sidewalks of New York? Once. But it's the only time I felt safe. I was badly drunk. In a bad drunk way.

DELIA

I'm familiar. Sick drunk.

DAN

Sick doesn't even begin. I saw signs, sidewalks, people veering out of my way. Taxis *avoiding* me. I fell off the curb—had no idea what it was—got up, staggered across the street wondering where all the *buildings* had gone—realized just as I got to the other side that probably I was crossing a street—looked around to confirm it, and fell over the other curb. (*Pause.*) In the rain. I remember walking up to a street light. I thought it was a street light, it wasn't a street light, I thought it was a street light, and wrapping my arms around it like it was my mother. Cold hard wet beautiful mother. Stood there forever. Long enough to lose all orientation. Finally opened my eyes and right at my nose this sign says: "You must answer to get help." (*Pause.*) White letters on a red field. "You must answer to get help." Blackout. Next thing I know, my roommate's shaking me awake asking me what time I got in. I said, "You must answer to get help." (*Pause.*) You ever see that sign? (*Pause.*) "You must answer . . ."

DELIA
I missed that one.

DAN
One on every block. I saw it about a month later. Old friend. Little letters: "Break glass; lift receiver; answer operator." Big print: "You *must* answer to get help." No more metaphysical than anything else in this world. (*Pause.*) Fire-alarm box. One on every block. (*Pause, looks at her.* DELIA *stares blankly off into space.*) Friend of man and dog. (*Long pause. He gets up, reaches for the lamp.*) Light on or off? (*Pause.*) Delia? D.K.? . . . light on or off?
(*A pause. He turns off light.* BLACKOUT.)

AUGUST
(*Slide: Mr. Jasker.*)
This is old man Jasker himself. The wise old bird who owns the place. After being made famous with the arrival of the college, he was looking forward to being made rich

by the arrival of the lake and Interstate 64. We see him twice each year, on our arrival and departure. This is a June hello—there was no September goodbye this summer. (*Slide: the moon.*) This is the moon.

(DELIA *is seated in the shadows.* CHAD *and* DAN *are noisily divesting themselves of rods, reels, creels, etc. Enjoying the noise; oblivious of the silence of the house.* DAN *goes to the refrigerator.*)

DAN
Nothing!

CHAD
Nothing?

DAN
Nothing to drink. Do you want to eat?

CHAD
God, no—

DAN
Food?

CHAD
Never again in my life.
(*He has found a bottle of Scotch.*)

DAN
Well, then there's nothing.

CHAD
You call that nothing?

DAN
Are you crazy; you want to kill yourself?

CHAD
No—you go. "Beer on whiskey—mightly." Mightly?

DAN
Mightly?

CHAD
What is it? You say it.

DAN
You're saying it. I don't know what—

CHAD
I'm telling you, it's an old wives' tale—there's a *thing*—a saying that tells you how to judge.

DAN
A what? What's the thing?

CHAD
A thing. You're the educated member of the family—you're supposed—

DAN
But not in FOLKLORE! Not in—

CHAD
I'm not talking—

DAN
—Absolute blind spot in folklore!

CHAD
I'm talking words—it's a epigram or epitaph or aphorism or anagram.

DAN
Axiom.

CHAD

It's not an axiom.

DAN

Well, what is it? Is it—

CHAD

It's not a goddamned axiom. It's an easy word—it's a word!
It's a saying—a truth!

DAN

That's the word. It's a truth.

CHAD

It's a truth, but that's not the word—ANYWAY!

DAN

Anyway. How does it go? Tell us! Are we safe? Will we
survive?

CHAD

It goes . . .
(*Pauses, trying to frame it.*)

DAN
(*Under*)
How does . . .

CHAD
(*Under*)
Just cool it a minute, will you? It goes: (*Headline*) "BEER.
ON WHISKEY."

DAN

Sounds bad.

CHAD

"MIGHTY RISKY . . . WHISKEY. ON BEER. NEVER FEAR."

DAN
(*Pause.*)
It's an aphorism.

CHAD
So. (*Pours a glass each.*) Whiskey on beer—
(*Toast.*)

DAN
Cheers.

CHAD
WHISKEY ON BEER . . .

DAN
That's what I said: "Never fear."

CHAD
Cheers.

(*They drink.*)

DAN
This will probably kill us.

CHAD
Hey! Have you ever seen anything as beautiful as that
moon?

DAN
Never.

CHAD
As big?

DAN
Never. When's the harvest moon?

CHAD
October.

DAN
Only the harvest moon.

CHAD
November.

DAN
Only the harvest moon.

CHAD
October.

DAN
Only the harvest moon.

CHAD
September.

DAN
As golden?

CHAD
Never.

DAN
What is it? June 21, 23—that's the summer solstice—moon.

CHAD
(*Simple*)
It's a full moon.

DAN
It's a full moon.

CHAD
And you're full of shit.

DAN
I'm fulla beer.

CHAD
I gotta piss.
(*He goes out the door.*)

DAN
(*Alone.*)
What'd we do?

CHAD
(*Off*)
Twelve.

DAN
Twelve's ass. I caught five and you caught what?

CHAD
(*Off*)
You caught five, I caught seven.

DAN
They be all right out in that tub?

CHAD
(*Off*)
You want to clean 'em?

DAN
Hell, I couldn't clean me.

CHAD
(*Off*)
You better manage it; Jean'll kick your ass out on the floor.

DAN

Hell she will. (*He stands, miming rod: casting, catch.*)
Strike! Shitfire! Strike! Get the net!

CHAD

(*Off*)
What?

DAN

Get the net, goddamnit, I got another one!

CHAD

(*Off*)
Get your own damn net; I got a seven-pounder out here.

DAN

(*Dropping it.*)
He who brags about size of meat— I forget what it was, but
Confucius said something very appropriate to that. What'll
it weigh? The big one. Five pounds?

CHAD

Six.

DAN

Was that one motherfuckin' fish? Was that a *fight?* To the
death?

CHAD

(*Entering.*)
That was a fight to the death.

DAN

Was that the biggest bass you ever saw in your life?

CHAD

No.

DAN
Shit.

CHAD
No.

DAN
You've seen a bigger bass?

CHAD
I've seen a bigger bass.

DAN
Drink your beer.

CHAD
I gotta get my ass home.

DAN
Would you drink your damn beer?

CHAD
You better get your duds off; get up to that warm bed, you're gonna be diggin' tomorrow.

DAN
Terrific. You know why? Cause what's happening is, it's all gone wrong. And that's always very terrific.

CHAD
Get up and have your girl give you a rubdown, huh?

DAN
Everything's looking like a typical village, right? And all of a sudden it's not typical any more. They got something under the roundhouse.

CHAD
Isn't that right?

DAN
We don't know what yet. What?

CHAD
You gotta get up to your girl.

DAN
She's beautiful, isn't she?

CHAD
She is that.

DAN
And bright—you wouldn't believe it.

CHAD
No, I'm counting on it. Let's take you up, put you to bed.

DAN
And sweet; you wouldn't believe it.

CHAD
No, I'm a believer.

DAN
You better believe it.

CHAD
Let's get you up to bed, come on.

DAN
I'm all wet.

CHAD
Come on.

DAN
I'm all wet, come on.

CHAD

Well, you said it.

DAN

Drink your—Scotch.

CHAD

Wore your life preserver, didn't you? That's nice out there, just you and me, huh?

DAN

Beautiful.

CHAD

Wouldn't be right with no one else, huh?

DAN

No way.

CHAD

You gettin' warm?

DAN

I'm fine.

CHAD

(*Very close to him.*)
You gonna be O.K.?

DAN

I am.

CHAD

(*Pulling him closer.*)
You sure? You sure?

DAN

Yeah, well, I didn't drown, I can survive without mouth-to-mouth resuscitation.

CHAD
Huh?

DAN
I'm fine.

CHAD
You know why you didn't drown—because you got a cork
head!

JEAN
(*Entering.*)
You've got to be kidding; it's one-thirty in the morning.

DAN
(*Whispering.*)
Oh, damn! NO! It's the night of nights! People should be
up.

JEAN
Do you drink when you're out fishing? No wonder people
go fishing. (*To* DELIA) Are you all right? I mean, are they
bothering you?

DELIA
Not at all.

DAN
Jesus Christ! I might have sat on you! We're all here. (*To*
JEAN, *moving toward her.*) This is the night—

JEAN
Shhh! The night of nights; I hear you. Come on, really.
I'm all over calamine lotion . . . I'm itching all—

DAN
(*Softly, singing, waltzing her gently a few steps.*)

Gently, gently, gently—"We're gonna fill an ocean of calamine lotion . . ."

JEAN
Come on, you'll wake me up; you'll wake me—(*Breaks
off.*) Oh, well, hell, it's too late; I'm awake. Damn. Damn.
Damn. Are you sure we won't bother you? Were you sleeping out here?

DELIA
No, you won't bother me. No, I wasn't sleeping.

JEAN
(*Opening refrigerator.*)
You hungry? I'm starved.

DAN
Is anybody hungry? No one is hungry.

DELIA
Whattaya say, Jasker?

JEAN
What are you drinking? Is that straight Scotch?

DAN
Well, yeah, it's . . . We're sipping.

CHAD
I'm gonna leave you all to your dig.

DAN
Stay. Stay.

CHAD
Later.
(*Leaving.*)

DAN

Stay awhile. (CHAD IS GONE.) Eat! We'll all eat! What's the matter with him?
(JEAN *is making a sandwich.*)

DELIA

What's he got on you?

DAN

Got on me? Nothing. What are you talking about, he's not got anything on me. I owe him my life—he's not got anything on me.

DELIA

Nobody owes their life to—

DAN

Well—some things you don't know, do you? He pulled me out of the drink last summer. We were rowing out; I was pulling back on the oar, it came out of the socket, hit me right in the face—I passed out and slid over the side in twenty feet of water.

JEAN

You're really too much.

DAN

Pulled me out by the hair of my head.

JEAN

What did you catch?

DAN

Oh! Incredible!

JEAN

Come on.

DAN
(*Whispers.*)
Four very friable, skillet-size bass. And one—mammoth . . .

DELIA
Motherfucking.

DAN
Motherfucking President of the Lake. Come and look!

JEAN
No, I haven't got any—

JEAN	DAN
—It's wet! I'm barefoot. I hate fish. I mean, I'll eat it, I'm glad you caught it, but I don't like live fish.	Come out and look. Come— Would you come out here and look.

DAN
What do you do when they got no sense of adventure?

JEAN
How big?

DAN
Very big. Formidable. Six pounds. If she hadn't been here, I'd of said twelve. But a fighter! A very . . . vicious opponent. Only six pounds, but solid muscle. Look at the moon at least—come look at the moon, you can see the moon from here; you don't have to even— where'd it go? (*He has taken her arm.*)

JEAN
You're soaking wet. Did you fall in?

DAN
I jumped in. I wanted to test my lifejacket.

JEAN
Did it work?

DAN
Uh . . . inconclusive. Anyway! I thought we were getting
a late start. I mean, what do I know, right? But it was hot.
And bass are hedonists. When it's hot on top they puddle
about down at the bottom, doing whatever they do when
it's hot on top. You got to know the psychology of the
mothers. To be a fisherman you have to be a kind of
amateur—

JEAN
Ichthyologist.

DAN
Ichthyopsychologist. But what do I know. So, no sign. We
row miles. Miles. (*Slowing down, tiring.* JEAN *has sat
down.*) You wouldn't believe the size of—there's one spot
that's surrounded—both sides—with pines. Miles and miles,
both sides. Anyway— (*Getting comfortable, against her, or
on her lap.* JEAN *continues to munch her sandwich.*) The
sun goes down. No big deal.

JEAN
No big deal.

DAN
A little rose, a little amber. Nothing to notice. Basic every-
day sundown. Then a bunch of disinterested strikes.

JEAN
Uninterested.

DAN

Uninterested strikes, all in a row. One two three four five six. So. There are fish in there; we just don't interest them much.

JEAN

Is this the fish or is this the moon?

DAN

Shhhh. This is the moon. This is the moon and the fish. This is both . . . We're busy with the strikes; we don't even notice it's getting dark. Another couple of strikes, nibbles—bait stealings—nothing serious. And all of a sudden it's night. Pitch. Ink. We're two hours away, easily. Might as well turn around. So we start back—and . . . up . . . drifts . . . this . . . orange. Deep orange . . . unstable . . . major moon. (*Beat.*) The lake is like . . .

JEAN

Glass.

DAN

. . . Very calm. We're rowing back—it's just beautiful. It's important. We stopped rowing and watched it. And then I threw my line in— (*Simply*) —just because we were stopping. And—"Galoompba." Immediately. (*Lying in her lap. Swaying with it.*) They swam up to that light like they were mesmerized by the light, dizzy on it . . .

JEAN

And that's when you caught them.

DAN

All—however many of them. Five and seven.

JEAN

Twelve.

DAN
All twelve of them.

JEAN
And by this time you were stoned.

DAN
Uhhh.

JEAN
Importantly stoned.

DAN
Uhhh.

JEAN
You bring back any grass?

DAN
Of course not.

JEAN
And what did you drink? (*Pause.. Shakes him lightly.*)
And what did you drink?

DAN
We drank . . . sunshine . . . and moonshine . . . and
the air . . . and trees . . . and singing . . . singing!
And fish . . . and comradery, and . . . (*Mentally
counts.*)
Five six-packs.

JEAN
You don't swim that well.

DAN
Chad swims like a duck.

JEAN

Ducks have rarely been known to save anyone from drowning more than once.

DAN

This is true. I'm going to go to bed. (*Gets up.*) Give me a kiss. (*Kisses her lightly.*) I'm going to go to bed. (*Exits.*)

JEAN

(*Pause.*)

I don't think I've ever been more awake. (*Pause.*) There's an old Chinese proverb: If you save someone from drowning, you're responsible for them for the rest of their life. I think Dan feels it's the other way around.

DELIA

I wasn't overly enthusiastic about the Orient.

JEAN

I'd like to see India. Japan.

DELIA

No, no . . . I couldn't take the Indian deities with their fucking Mona Lisa smiles saying: "Well, that's for us to know and you to find out." I made the only rationalization possible. I decided they didn't know at all. Come drift with me on a raft in the sea of tranquillity. I'd go nuts. All of which would have served me very well if I could have forgotten it was a rationalization.

JEAN

Don't you make yourself tired with all that?

DELIA

(*Profound sigh; pause.*)

Yes.

JEAN

I mean, they're only pieces of sculpture. They're art objects. They're not Shiva and Shakti themselves. Shakti didn't come down and sit for her portrait. She didn't pose for the artist.

DELIA

(*Beat.*)

I believe she did. I think that she did. You're not easily quailed by the inscrutable.

JEAN

Inscrutable. In. I-N, in. Scrut. S-C-R-U-T, scrut. Inscrut. Ah. A, ah. Inscruta—ble. B-L-E, ble. Inscrutable. Inscrutable: I-N-S-C-R-U-T-A-B-L-E, inscrutable.

(CYNTHIA, *in a robe, comes down, mildly surprised to see them. She hesitates only a second, then, without thinking further about it, crosses the room to the back door and lets herself out. They watch but do not comment.*)

DELIA

(*After a moment*)

Men. God, they're sad—depressing poor bastards, breaking their balls for their families. We're their reflection, I suppose, but I don't know as they love us for it. (AUGUST *enters, goes to the refrigerator, looks in.*) Who would have the time? I wonder, do we drive them to it?

JEAN

Women?

(AUGUST *takes a bottle of milk from the refrigerator, sets it on a table, goes for a glass, leaving the refrigerator door open.*)

DELIA

No. Wives. I have an odd vision that women are wonderful. It's the wives. Sad old wives. (AUGUST *pours milk into the glass, and sits at the table staring off.*) I wouldn't be a man. Not and carry the dumbfounding load they've saddled themselves with. Actually, now that I think of it, being a woman is worse. We're the remains. We're what's left. We're the lees in the bottom of the bottle. You know how the world ends? You know what the "with a whimper" is? A sad old world of widows: wizened old women, lined up on beaches along all the Southern coastlines looking out over the water and trying to keep warm. (*Beat.*) Good Lord. That sounds so horribly right I'll bet it's prophetic. The species crawls up out of the warm ocean for a few million years and crawls back to it again to die. Why don't you make me a drink.

JEAN

No.

(AUGUST *notices the light from the refrigerator, returns the bottle, closes the refrigerator door.* BLACKOUT.

A flashlight beam moves slowly across the stage, investigating the chairs, the refrigerator, the floor. The light goes out. We hear the screen door creak and close. A pause.)

END OF FIRST ACT

ACT 2

(Everyone except KIRSTEN *is onstage,* DAN *presiding.)*

DAN
Well, it's wrong is what it is. It's all wrong. Show her the Polaroid.

CYNTHIA
(Handing JEAN *a print.)*
You won't be able to tell much.

AUGUST
Burials have a way of turning up just as the light goes.

JEAN
I can't tell a thing from this.

DAN
(Looking over her shoulder.)
See, he's laid out straight, head to the right.

JEAN
He isn't missing a hand, by any chance?

DAN
No, he's got the usual number of hands and three feet. Which is kinda funny when you see it.

CYNTHIA
Very awkward for dancing.

JEAN
Are you going to play with me, or are you going to tell me what you've found?

CYNTHIA
The third foot is incursive from some neighbor.

DAN
We don't know what we've found until we go over and see who his buddy is, and how many of them there are.

AUGUST
Tomorrow.

DAN
You're damn right.

CYNTHIA
Come out tomorrow, you might actually see August with a trowel in his hand.

DAN
Something's up; it's all wrong. Remember the roundhouse I showed you? With the fire in the middle? Well, these guys are buried under the roundhouse.

AUGUST
Looks almost as if the house was built over them.

JEAN
And that's not cricket.

DAN
Uh—no. That's not cricket.

JEAN
Does he have artifacts around him?

DAN
Very low caste. Not so much as a little stone pipe.

JEAN
You think they had a caste system?

CYNTHIA
All the latest advancements.

DAN
As a matter of fact, around 1500 a tribe called the Natchez
ended up down in Mississippi, where the French settlers
studied them for about fifty years, decided they were dangerous, and rubbed them out—

JEAN
—Oh, God—

DAN
—Exactly. And it looks like the Natchez might have been
the last of the Mound Builders. Hey, Deek—want to write
a book? *Last of the Mound Builders*—I'd be glad to advise
for a small consideration.

DELIA
Delia or D.K. Not "Deek."

DAN
So. If our guys were anything like the Natchez, they had a
really off-the-wall, really bizarre, caste system.

AUGUST
Four distinct castes: The Suns—

DAN
—who were the very big muck-a-mucks, led by the Great
Sun, who was a god-king.

AUGUST
Then the Nobles, then the Honored Men, and then the
Stinkards.

DAN

Really. Stinkards. Or that's the French translation. And of course most everybody was a Stinkard.

CYNTHIA

So things haven't changed all that much.

AUGUST

—and the Suns, the Nobles, and the Honored Men could only marry into the Stinkard class, with the second generation assuming the class of the mother. So only someone with a Sun mother and a Stinkard father could become the new God-King.

DAN

And everybody married Stinkards. Including the other Stinkards.

CYNTHIA

I didn't realize that.

AUGUST

I thought probably you did.

DAN

So they were an "upward-mobile," matriarchal society with a god-king muck-a-muck. All dressed in swan feathers. Carried on a litter everywhere he went. Like Delia; huh, D.K.?

DELIA

Dan, it has been years since I've dressed in swan feathers.

JEAN

How long did they live? Not the Natchez, our guys.

DAN

Short.

JEAN
How long? How short?

AUGUST
If they reached the age of fifteen, their life expectancy was maybe thirty.

(*A light thunder is heard, and gradually a wind rises.*)

DAN
Do not ask how old I'll be my next birthday.

CYNTHIA
You haven't reached the age of fifteen.

JEAN
And won't. The head of the department calls him "Polly-andy" to his face.

AUGUST
The head of the department is an extremely nihilistic individual.

DAN
This is true.

JEAN
What did they eat?

DAN
(*Who has gone back to studying drawings of the grave site.*)
Huh? Oh—corn, squash, beans—

CHAD
That's succotash.

DAN

You kill, right? When you can't flunk 'em? They ate everything. Shellfish, deer . . .

CHAD

For all you know, they were cannibals.

DAN

Of course; you know, I'd love to discover they were cannibals. Only I doubt if we'd ever be funded again. They had
fairly elaborate ritualistic human sacrifices, but they
weren't barbarians.

CYNTHIA

Actually, there's evidence that they did practice cannibal-
ism.

DAN

None. Here? None. You're talking about Wisconsin. The
people of southern Illinois are certainly not responsible
for the perverted table manners of the people of Wisconsin. I personally wouldn't be surprised at anything that
was discovered in Wisconsin. I think there's something in
the water that twists their minds.

CHAD

Beer.

DAN

Very likely. Exactly.

AUGUST

Is that rain?

DAN

Is it raining? Damn. I better go down and see that they got
everything covered. (*Getting a slicker.*) Let up already.
(*Going out.*) My God, it's pouring.

JEAN
Put the hood up.

DAN
(*Off*)
What?

JEAN
Your hood, dummy. Put the hood up.

(*Several slides of rain and the lake.*)

AUGUST
(*Isolated by the light to his desk area.*)
Up, up, up, up. Every morning Dr. Loggins pushed a stake
into the edge of the lake, trying, I think, to kill it. And
every evening the lake had covered it. Nine tributaries
empty into the basin, draining almost all of two coun-
ties. By the time the lake overran the site, it didn't at all
matter.

(CHAD *knocks at the door. After a moment,* JEAN *comes
down.*)

CHAD
I've been wanting to talk to you.

JEAN
(*After an audible sigh.*)
I think maybe if you didn't come here . . . I mean, I
know it's your house, and Dan likes you, you're a terrific
relief from his gaggle of volunteers, but—you're putting
yourself through something that seems so unnecessary.

CHAD
I thought we should talk. Just with nobody—

JEAN

We're talking, I don't mind; I'm perfectly willing to talk,
but you can't expect it to be the sort of talk—

CHAD

(*Overlapping from "expect," letting himself in.*)
What? Are you trying to make a fool of me? We're not
talking; I got my boat over here. We'll go over to the
place, the six acres I told you about—it's gonna be an
island when the lake fills, I want to show you. There's a
cave. It's going to be under water in another couple of
days . . .

JEAN

(*A long pause.*)
No.

CHAD

I thought you said we'd talk.

JEAN

Say whatever it is you want to say. It won't improve with
the change in scene.

CHAD

It's just down at the landing—

JEAN

You have some kind of romantic fantasy going on that
frankly frightens—

CHAD

I gave it a paint job; you ought to look at it.

JEAN

Chad, for godsake, I don't even swim, I don't like water,

I don't like boats, it's pouring rain, and I'm not at all attracted to you.

CHAD

You don't know anything about me, you don't know—

JEAN

That is absolutely true, but I can live with it. You said you wanted to talk; you don't want to talk, you want to bludgeon. I'm married to a guy you claim is your friend— I'm going— I'm very much committed to him— I'm really sorry, but you make me feel foolish.

CHAD

O.K., O.K., O.K., you don't want to be with just me. Maybe what you want is for the three of us to get together. Go out fishing . . .

JEAN
(*Going.*)
You're too much of a sport for me, Chad, you're too sporty for me.

CHAD

I thought you said we'd talk.

JEAN

Please put it out of your head, I don't like it. You make me uncomfortable.

CHAD

You said we'd talk. (AUGUST *enters with* KIRSTEN.) Bitch of a day, huh?

AUGUST
(*Shaking water from his hat.*)
None too bright. (CHAD *exits.*) I don't know, Jean—I

think it's not a good idea to socialize too much with our
little surrogate landlord.

JEAN

Socialize?— Dan seems to like him.

AUGUST

Well, Dan, for all his ebullience, is quite tactful really.

JEAN

And I'm not—or women aren't.

DAN
(*Entering soaked.*)
Brother! Drowned.

JEAN

You really are. (*Hands him a towel.*) You get the girls
into the motel?

DAN

Yeah, their tents were almost washing out from under
them; they're game, but they're stupid. The lake is insane;
it's ten feet higher than it's supposed to be—if it's raining
tomorrow, we're going to have to work anyway.

JEAN

You get dried off?

DAN

Yeah, I'm fine.

KIRSTEN
(*At the table*)
What's in the sifter?

DAN

Seeds.

KIRSTEN
Maize? (*Pause.*) Maize?

DAN
Grass. *Cannabis sativa.*

KIRSTEN
Oh.

(DELIA, *dressed in a clean robe, walks unsteadily but unaided down the stairs.*)

DAN
Well. It walks, it talks. It takes nourishment from a spoon.

(AUGUST *moves into the office.*)

DELIA
Spiritually it still crawls on its belly like a reptile.—And it no longer takes nourishment from a spoon.

JEAN
You didn't.

DAN
You know the Contemporary Lit. professor I told you about? Used to read your stuff out loud?

DELIA
(*Sits.*)
Don't push.

DAN
Thought of his name. Dr. Landau. Had a great voice. Said—what do you think about this?—said—

DELIA
I don't want to know what he said.

DAN
No, you'll get a kick out of it.

JEAN
This is about which one, this is *Spindrift?*

DAN
Yeah, said you were checking off the possibilities of the species. You know, if it hadn't been for the—

DELIA
That's such a load of crap, what a load of—you know what I wrote? How I teased myself through it? I set a simple problem and tried to solve it. Write a Chinese puzzle box. Write a Russian doll. A box within a box within a box within a box. Every time something was solved, within the solution was another problem, and within the solving of the second riddle another question arose. And when that riddle was unwound there was still a knot. And you know why I failed? For me? Because either a Chinese puzzle box must go on *ad infinitum* or there must finally be a last box. And when that box is opened, something must finally be in it. Something simple like maybe an answer. Or a fact, since we all seem to be compulsive compilers. Look at you, digging your evidence, piecing together shards, fragments, sherds. Clues, footnotes, artifacts, pollen grains, bones, chips.

DAN
(Overlapping from "pollen grains")
Not of themselves—in association. Where are they, why are they there?

DELIA
Boxes in boxes.

DAN
(*Simultaneously overlapping second "boxes"*)
Boxes in boxes. And when you got all the knots unwound
in your book, and all the problems untied, and got down
to the final little box—

DELIA
The Russian doll.

DAN
and it was opened, what was inside?

DELIA
(*Pause.*)
Another book.

DAN
(*Pause.*)
I didn't know there was another . . .

DELIA
Well, that shows what you know. I thought it should be
for Dad. A simple . . . simple . . . Then, of course, Dad
died, and I—
(*Pause.*)

JEAN
What?

DELIA
"In Memoriam" never interested me much.

DAN
(*Softly*)
There wasn't another . . .

DELIA

For you to see? For Dr. Landau to read aloud? I heard it—
I saw it down there somewhere . . . that graceful, trim,
and dangerous leviathan that got away—it moved in the
cold depths of some uncharted secret currents where the
sun has never warmed the shadows. Graceful and taunting.
Moving through a spectrum of dark colors alien to the unaided eye. I could have captured it and displayed to the
light some undiscovered color. But it was deaf to my
charms and tokens and incantations. I called the son of a
bitch, but it wouldn't rise. So I went down to find it.

DAN
(Pause.)
And it got away . . .

DELIA
(Laughs.)
Well, I didn't get away. It caught me!

DAN
Tell me about—

DELIA
Tell me about the three-footed skeleton you've found.

DAN
We can't work, Delia; how can we work in this?
(Goes to office door.)

AUGUST
If it's this bad tomorrow, we'll put up tarps.

JEAN
I've thought about that house you grew up in. Big old
masculine rooms with medical charts.

DELIA

Oak floors and old oak furniture. And light. The whole place filled with sunlight. Especially in the winter.

AUGUST

She left when she was seventeen; I'm surprised she'd tell anyone about it.

DELIA

I'm the one who liked it, so I'm the one who remembers it.

AUGUST

I never said I didn't like it.

DELIA

He liked it so much he sold it the first week he could. Without mentioning to me that it was up for sale—

AUGUST

You were being sick in Mexico, as I recall, and couldn't come to the funeral.

JEAN

Boy, you two make me glad I'm an only child and grew up with grandparents.

AUGUST

It's all quite past. That's all past. Water under the bridge. Water under the bridge.

DAN

Water, water, water, water, water—

(*Slide of bone awl.*)

AUGUST

This bone awl you might as well enter as made by one Mr. Cochise Mississippi, around A.D. 1100.

DAN
(*Overlapping*)
Mississippian; around A.D. 1100, give or take fifty years;
it's made from a turkey metacarpal bone.

JEAN
You get into some far-afield studies, don't you?

DAN
Umm.

AUGUST
Most everything we're finding here is remarkably well
preserved.

(CYNTHIA *enters.*)

DELIA
(*Handing the bone awl to* JEAN.)
Well, that's a real keen bone awl, Cochise, but what have
you done recently?

CYNTHIA
More recently they vanished without a trace. Along with
the whole Mississippian Culture.

DELIA
Along with nearly everyone; vanished without a trace.

DAN
(*Still leaning against the screen, watching the rain.*)
Vanished without a trace, vanished without a trace, van-
ished without a trace. God, I wish it would stop raining.
Vanished without a trace. Nine mounds and a hothouse do
not constitute without a trace. We've seen the outline of

the foundations of houses used for gentlemen's clubs, complete with fireplace, never mind the ventilation. Vanished without a trace. It happens that this awl is one of the finest-crafted utilitarian tools discovered in North America—Cochise did not disappear without a trace. I think we have palpable evidence of his craft, of a subtle skill and imagination, of his care and conscientiousness. I think with his example his family stood proud and neat. I think his wife fashioned for him quilled buckskin aprons and kilts of surpassing brilliance that dazzled the tribe. Past? Vanished? Without a trace? Cochise? His passing, women, was mourned by tribes up and down the length of this river. I think his friends told histories around the fire of his craftiness in trapping game. Women cried and brave warriors walked out into the woods to be alone and fathom his loss. I think odes were composed and spoken and learned and repeated down the generations; songs were sung. I think so sure and strong a warrior stood as an example that young braves and children held up to themselves; I think Cochise was extraordinary beyond precedent. He danced with grace, he bathed twice a day, he spoke with simplicity and truth, and nursed the sick back to strength; he tamed wild animals and laughed when the children were frightened at night. I think he spread his arms out in an open field in the sun and yellow-green parakeets that he had tamed to sit on his hands came when he called them. I think wolves nuzzled his thighs and allowed him to walk in the wild as their comrade a thousand years before anyone named Francis walked in Assisi! Goddamn this rain!

(*He grabs his slicker, kicks the screen door open, and charges out into the rain.*)

JEAN

Put the hood up! (*Pause.*) I have a feeling he really be-
lieves that. If it weren't for August, nothing they write
would ever get published.

CYNTHIA

If it weren't for Dan, the work wouldn't get done in the
first place.

DELIA

Parakeets?

CYNTHIA

Don't get him started. Parakeets were as common in
Illinois as the sparrow is now.

JEAN

They weren't tropical?

DELIA

Some things we don't know, huh?

AUGUST

We have no clear idea what the bone awl was actually used
for, but it was undoubtedly used for something. This is a
particularly good one.
(*He goes into the office.*)

CYNTHIA

Chad Jasker said he'd drive me into town; I think he's
changed my plans.

JEAN

He was—

DELIA

I just left him standing on every corner; all the Mediterranean youths are hustlers.

CYNTHIA
Hustlers? I don't know why you call him a hustler. The Mediterraneans are probably poor, and he's poor.

DELIA
Not by their standards he isn't. Poor hustlers, rich hustlers—

CYNTHIA
You talk about how rich they're going to be—

JEAN
They are though—

CYNTHIA
Oh, they are not.

JEAN
No, really. When the lake comes in, God, they own about a mile of the shoreline.

CYNTHIA
Poor people don't become rich. It takes capital to develop a lakeshore—they're rich with fantasy. They'll sell for what they think is money and be ripped off. They're not going to be rich.

JEAN
To hear him tell it, it's settled. You've heard about the Holiday Inn and all that . . . the place is going to be a spa . . . they're sitting right in the middle of it.

CYNTHIA
I'm sure they'll borrow from the usurers and have the whole property extorted out from under them.

DELIA
I was only thinking, there are those who hustle and those
who don't.

CYNTHIA
There are winners and losers, givers and takers; there's
the quick and the dead; Chad tries to be among the quick.
Sometimes it shows. What are you? Or do you know?

DELIA
I'm a nomad.

CYNTHIA
And you're happy with that?

DELIA
Happy has nothing to do with it, Cynthia.

CYNTHIA
Well, it sure as hell wouldn't seem to.

DELIA
(*Pause. Friendly*)
If it applied, I could ask you the same thing: Are you
happy with that? But it doesn't apply.

CYNTHIA
(*Backing down.*)
Forgive me for bringing it up. There are things I need
that you perhaps don't.

DELIA
We all need them. It's a question of what you're willing
to pay.

CYNTHIA
Well. You're willing to pay a good deal more than I am.

JEAN
No. She isn't.

DELIA
I'm used to shopping in bargain basements, peasant
bazaars. You're paying the gold of the realm for bazaar
merchandise.

CYNTHIA
All that glitters . . .

JEAN
I don't believe that.

CYNTHIA
(*Letting it pass.*)
I thought you had given up on men. Wasn't there some
woman sculptor or someone?

DELIA
Good God, no. Never. I know—I should have. A long time
ago; I just never got around to it. Isn't it pathetic, it's too
late to change.

JEAN
I don't think I could get into it. (*They laugh.*) Is that
funny? I guess it is. Wasn't there a story about you and
some woman? About tearing up some bar?

DELIA
Which bar?

JEAN
In Spain or somewhere. Oh, no! You were fighting. You
were arrested.

DELIA
Not in Spain; I'd still be there.

JEAN
Did you know you made all the newspapers?

DELIA
Of course I knew. Why do you think I did it?

CYNTHIA
They used to call us for comments; we hadn't heard from
her in four years.

DELIA
Now no one has. That was Cannes, Nice . . . along that
winding, cliff-hanging—in a Mazerati. That was P.R. That
wasn't me. A couple of times I allowed myself to cause a
brawl or pass out in the middle of the ring because I
knew it was good for the biographer. If there's such a
thing as sin any more, that must be high on the list. Which
of the commandments would that come under? It's not
really so bad to lie; sometimes it's kinder. Go ahead and
steal, really, most of the bastards deserve to lose it. But
I've "sinned." I've humiliated myself because people ex-
pected it of me.

CYNTHIA
(*Closing the refrigerator in disgust.*)
Christ, this house is crammed with drugs. Doesn't anybody
drink any more?

(BLACKOUT.)

AUGUST
Dianne, would you just note marginally that I have decided I am definitely sick of aesthetics. Aesthetics and all
the representatives of the humanities ransacking anthro-
pological collections for pots they find pleasingly shaped

and carrying them off to museums, where they lecture
without content on form—and without the least ethnologi-
cal information or understanding. Aesthetics is becoming
an enemy to thought. (*Pause. Slide: college graduation.*)
What the hell is— Christ, this is my graduation—notice the
innocent and hopeful countenance. Prepared to conquer
lost worlds with a doctorate in one hand and a trowel in
the other. (*Slide:* DAN—*a pause.*) A man's life work is
taken up, undertaken, I have no doubt, to blind him to
the passing moon. I have no doubt that in an area of his
almost unconscious he knows this and therefore is not
blinded but only driven. The dig at Jasker's Field was un-
finished. A salvage operation from which we salvaged
nothing. Slides of picnics, slides of houses, slides of water,
slides of ducks, slides of boats, slides of pain, slides of need,
slides of spear points. A great amount of work has been
done on the early cultures of North America and we have
found only the periphery of the culture. Three hundred
mounds, numberless graves have been opened, usually
seconds before the builders plowed them under. And of
the Mississippian Culture—never before had the grave of
a god-king been discovered. The most important find in
forty years of work. We do not allow ourselves to dream of
finding what we might find and dream every sweep of a
trowel. And what is salvaged? Nothing. Nothing. (*To the
slides*) Nothing. Nothing. Nothing. Nothing. Nothing.
Nothing.

(JEAN *and* DELIA *are reading. There are approaching
sounds of girls yelling, everyone yelling,* DAN's *voice heard
approaching. They stand as he enters. The slides continue
flicking repeatedly across the screen.*)

DAN

Jean, Jean, Jean, Jean— Come out—come down—the muck-a-muck. The high and holy muck-a-muck—

JEAN

—What? Who is it? In the grave?—

DAN

Not one—I'll be very calm, I'm not trembling, shit, I'm fine— We started clearing away toward the third foot—you remember the—grave, the—

JEAN

—Sure, sure . . . The Stinkard—

DAN

—Third foot? He isn't a Stinkard, he's a retainer, dozens of them—all over the place—and in the center the ground is dark—a big black square where there has been a log tomb. It's all rotted away, but the ground is dark. August said, Oh, my God. Oh, my God. It's the tomb of a god-king. Nobody's ever found— (*Breathes deeply.*) You have never seen anything like it. Never. We didn't know if they had gold—but a gold thing on his face—and copper— Beautiful copper breastplates—everywhere—pearls like—obsidian axes, beads, thousands of tons of—come on. Delia, if you don't come out and see this, I'll never read another word you— I swear to you, two more days and the lake would have flooded it. We're going to have to break our asses.

JEAN

A muck-a-muck? A god-king?

DAN

Oh, God, what a god he must have been! Pottery. *Glazed*
pots—fifty, sixty of them. It's going to be dark in no time;
hurry up, it's soaking wet—we're up to our knees— Oh, my
God, how famous we're going to be! You gotta write the
book, Delia, you really gotta write it.

DELIA

I'll come down and see. If I can't make it, I expect to be
carried on the muck-a-muck's litter.

DAN

I'll carry you on my back.

JEAN

Pearls?

DAN

A room full—and maybe *gold*. This mask thing. We
thought they might have gold. They had trade routes into
country where there's gold. Copper armbands, bracelets. I
am perfectly calm. I am a mature and balanced scientist.
I wish you could see August up to his ass in mud. He said,
"This is a very high muck-a-muck." (DELIA *and* JEAN *hurry
off.*) What am I supposed to get? I was supposed to get
something.

(AUGUST, CHAD, CYNTHIA, JEAN, DELIA, *and* KIRSTEN, *all
carrying boxes, overrun him, pass back and forth, busy
with things, working, tired and high, but preoccupied.*
KIRSTEN *goes upstairs.*)

CYNTHIA

Pitch black, it's absolutely maddening. You know you're
not going to keep it under your hat.

AUGUST
For a while; for a day.

CYNTHIA
(*To* CHAD)
You're pledged, you know that—not a word. Because if it
gets out, it's all over; we'll have to set up guards.

CHAD
You could get lights, you could work at night—

AUGUST
That would be subtle.

DAN
We'd draw a larger crowd than the World Series.

AUGUST
You called Croff?

CYNTHIA
Yes, again. You want to know what he said again? (*They
go back to working—she tells the women.*) He pissed. He
was absolutely wetting his pants. He kept saying, Where's
August? I said, he's down at the goddamned dig, where
would you be? He started looking up charter-plane com-
panies. I said, Croff, don't sweat it, we won't be doing anything until it gets light; drive down in the morning. He's
already calculating the size of the grant the college will be
getting from this. He has his picture on the cover of *News-
week*. He honest-to-God asked me when *Scientific American* went to press.

DAN
Jasker's the one who's going to be famous, you know that,
don't you?

(*As the work organizes itself,* DAN *is painting green copper beads with nail polish;* AUGUST *is cleaning something as delicately as an artist;* CYNTHIA *is writing the location and date numbers on projectile points, pottery shards, and small envelopes of pearls;* JEAN *is entering the numbers on a chart.*)

CYNTHIA
It's going to be the most important archaeological dig in America.

DAN
Well, north of the Rio.

CHAD
You know, no bull, I admire you people. You're really trying to make something of yourself. You could have been on vacation like everybody else. I'd just make a bet—you're not doing it for what you get. I've watched you down there and I wouldn't have the patience for it.

CYNTHIA
They wouldn't have the patience to bust down a transmission or any of the tinkerings that—

CHAD
—No, you do that 'cause you got to do it; 'cause you'd be embarrassed not to. But, see—you guys are finding little pieces of charcoal last week and stuff if I saw on the ground I wouldn't bother to bend down for, but now that you found something—what's something in that grave that's valuable? I mean, that you could sell?

CYNTHIA
Almost everything.

DAN

—No more hitches with funding, you realize that. We'll be turning people down.

AUGUST

Well, now, no point in being high-handed.

CHAD

If someone came along and offered you—where's the thing? The gold thing? The bead?

DAN

Jean?

JEAN

On the table.

CHAD

See? Sitting on the table. If someone offered to buy this—

AUGUST

Very carefully, Mr. Jasker. That's the first gold ever—

CHAD

I know, I watched you with it. How much would you ask for that, how much is that worth?

AUGUST

(*Carefully*)

The gold in it—is worth maybe two or three dollars. It's beaten very thin and spread around a wooden bead. The wood has long since disintegrated. (*Taking it.*) You can hear it rattle inside. You felt how light it was.

CHAD

See, two dollars. You'd only ask what it was really worth—you wouldn't try to make anything for— Like what you really want to know is—aw, no—well—

AUGUST
I suppose if we knew that—

CHAD
(*Over*)
No, forget I said it, I can't say it; I'm not saying it right; I don't know what I'm trying to say. What are these?

AUGUST
(*Taking them from him.*)
Why do you come here?

CHAD
(*Beat.*)
Beg pardon, Doc? Whatta you mean?

AUGUST
You could be any number of places.

CYNTHIA
We undoubtedly have our attractions, August.

AUGUST
You were down at the dig last week watching the excavation of a fire pit. Charcoal and split rocks. Anyone could see there was no intrinsic material value in that find.

CHAD
Yeah, I know, but it's—

AUGUST
You asked when it had been built, how old it was—which were the precise questions we were asking ourselves.

CHAD
No, I'm not putting it right.

AUGUST

People are drawn to speculate. Even my sister, who has no curiosity about anything—

DAN

I'm going to get her to write us up, though. Fictionalized, of course.

AUGUST

I think archaeology can survive without that.

CHAD

Now you got your boss impressed; he's going to be down—

DAN

Something like this, we need people to verify that we aren't faking it—it's—

AUGUST

(*Minimizing.*)
He's the sort that likes to check up on his employees. He's come down a number of times. Generally unannounced.

CHAD

I gotta have another beer. See, that's why I come here; I can always count on Dan to turn me on.

CYNTHIA

Oh, I think you can be turned on by any number of things.

AUGUST

(*He lifts from the table the fragile gold mask he has been cleaning.*)
Look at this, coming out beautifully.

CYNTHIA
(*Getting her camera and a flash unit.*)
I want to get this.

DAN
It's a death mask—we guess. It might have had feathers
around it here. We have to guess. We've never seen anything like it before. (*He holds it up to his face, and almost inadvertently it stays in place.*) Is that incredible?
Tell me I look like a god-king.

JEAN
Don't put that—

DAN
I didn't do a thing.

CYNTHIA
Smile. Or can you?
(*Flash.*)

DAN
Let me see. I'm blind. Help me with it. (AUGUST *carefully
lifts it from* DAN's *face.*) That's the same design we've seen
on gorgets, and assumed it was meant to represent pig-
mentation.

CHAD
That thing's solid gold, isn't it?

AUGUST
(*A lie.*)
That's copper—they valued it above gold.

DAN
It's fragile as hell. He didn't wear it, you know—they made

it for him after he died. If you can imagine it completely surrounded with feathers.

JEAN

I really didn't like it on you at all.

DAN

Are you crazy; every dead god-king is wearing one this year. It may take a while to catch on.

CHAD

These are beads; they're copper too?

DAN

Those will fall right apart, Chad, they're corroded right through. They're made the same as the gold—they beat out a solid nugget of copper—they had no metallurgical knowledge, to speak of.

CYNTHIA

What have you got all over your hands?

CHAD

Oh, that's uh—paint; got more on me than I did on the car.

CYNTHIA

You painted your car?

DELIA

It's a different car.

CHAD

Got a new one; painted it black. I had 'em put on the papers that it was black, it was some kind of green, all rusted off; I had to paint it before I got stopped.

CYNTHIA

You sold the blue one?

CHAD
Wrapped it up.

CYNTHIA
The Olds?

CHAD
Couple a days ago, over on 14.

DAN
He wraps it around a tree, gets out, leaves it there, and hitches a lift home.

CHAD
Sheriff comes by, says they towed it to the dump, tried to give me a summons for abandoning it. I told him I was dazed; I didn't know what I was doing . . .

DAN
How'd you know it was a different car?

DELIA
I'm familiar with all possible transportation in and out of here.

JEAN
What's that stuff you're putting on that?

DAN
Just nail polish, help hold it together.

JEAN
Smells vile.

DAN
You look tired; don't get sick again.

CHAD
You been sick?

JEAN
No. Woozy; tired, not sick.

DAN
I think she's developing evening sickness. You've heard of morning sickness; she's getting evening sickness.

JEAN
(*To* CYNTHIA)
Did you have that?

CYNTHIA
Boring as hell, isn't it?

CHAD
What from?

DAN
Who knows the metabolism of a pregnant woman? She'll feel better tomorrow; she can diagnose what was wrong with her and write a paper on it.

JEAN
Might do it too.

CHAD
Since when was you—
(*A long pause. His face registers the implication of the statement. They do not notice and continue working.*)

AUGUST
(*To* DAN)
What are you hiding there?

(DAN *gives him a box, which* AUGUST *begins to sort through.*)

CHAD
(*Finally. Pinched*)
When's it due?

DAN
December, January.

CHAD
Hell, probably ought to celebrate.

DAN
Thought I told you.

CHAD
Not me.

DAN
As big as the hole is in the gold bead, what would you
think—these are all small—if several ropes of copper beads
came down like this and then the strings went through the
gold one.

AUGUST
Where's the Polaroid of his chest; how was the copper
situated?

CYNTHIA
(*Overlapping* DAN *from "gold bead."*)
What did you say you were going to show me on your car?

CHAD
Me?

CYNTHIA
I don't know; you said you had something in the trunk.

CHAD
Trunk's locked. I don't have the key for it.

CYNTHIA
Maybe it was the hood, I don't know.

CHAD
I think you're thinking of someone else.

CYNTHIA
(*Going out the door.*)
Well, anyway, I want to see this famous paint job.

CHAD
I ain't got time. I gotta get going. (*Steps outside a second.*)
Leave me alone.

CYNTHIA
(*Goes to the refrigerator, gets out a beer.*)
Anyone else? Auggie?

AUGUST
I'm fine.

CHAD
(*Finally. Hardly audible, but hard*)
Whatta you gonna call it? (*As* JEAN, *who has heard, starts to leave*) HEY! (*Everyone freezes.*) Said, what name you gonna name it?

DAN
What?

CHAD
(*Almost in tears*)
The baby.

DAN
We're taking all suggestions, putting them in a hat.

CHAD

What then, you'll pull it out like a rabbit? It's no more important to you than that?

DAN

Well, we figure when we have a palpable, honest-to-God kid, with a gender, we'll think of something.

(KIRSTEN *comes down, hangs back at the stairs.*)

CHAD

Boy, you guys are supercool, supercool. Down here in the sticks, you got your little harem of ugly girl students around you watching every little brush stroke and pick and pry like you was painting the world's last masterpiece. You got your pretty wives and your kids and your drug-addict sister. You really got everything going for you. Cynthia says you're going to be getting write-ups in *Time* magazine.

CYNTHIA

I said Croff envisions his mug on the cover.

CHAD

You got the place all tied up so anything you find belongs to you. You're really knocking it.

AUGUST

That was the agreement your father signed.

CHAD

(*Not hearing*)

I really got to admire your supercool.

DAN

We got it knocked.

CHAD

You really got it knocked. You're digging up all these old battle weapons— (*Lifting from the box a foot-long spear point.*) Just look at the craftsmanship on that—what'd you say that was? You called that a spear point. Who'd think those old boys would have the tools to make something like that.

AUGUST

That's very dangerous.

CYNTHIA

You said you had to be somewhere by—

CHAD

Hell, you don't even need—you can break someone's neck just by putting the right twist in the right place. (*He has, as quick as a snake, reached around* CYNTHIA'*s neck with his arm.*) You know that?

CYNTHIA

I'm sure you could. You're a lot stronger than I.

(*He releases her.*)

CHAD

It's a damn shame you're going to have to find yourself some other field of operation.

DAN

We'll be a while on this one yet.

CHAD

I'm talking about next year.

DAN

Next year we can get back to those mounds you think are so important.

CHAD

I guess you can if you can find where the road-construction crew scatters them. Only I don't think the Holiday Inn people are going to much appreciate a scruffy gang of ugly virgins digging up the front yard of their motel.

CYNTHIA

I don't know why you think they're virgins.

DAN

People eating at your restaurant?

CHAD

You think it's cute? You think it's not going to happen? There are some cost accountants and some professional architects from down at Memphis you should talk to.

DAN

The tourists are going to be flooding the place heavier than the lake, huh?

CHAD

You may know a hell of a lot about your grave robbing but you're really full of shit when it comes to commerce. I know you've had your nose stuck in the ground; it's not easy to see what's going on around you from that position, but this is the last trip you fellows are making down here—

DAN

—You don't seem to realize the importance of what's happened here today. Coordinating this site with the information we're going to be getting from the mounds— The information we have already will take years—

CHAD
(*Overlapping from "we have"*)
You're just going to have to go on what you've got, buddy.

DAN
—It's a man's life work here—

CHAD
'Cause as it happens, I don't want you here. And there ain't going to be any mounds. The mounds are going to be fucking flat. The mounds are going to be under about forty tons of highway interchange. They're going to be under a tennis court.

DAN
I mean, it doesn't matter whether you understand or not, but I'd think you'd want to be part of that. Goddamn! If you want tourists coming in here, we're going to have to be digging around them.

DAN
I don't want to hear about your tennis courts.

CHAD
You people are dreaming! You might not like it, but there ain't no mounds next year. There's an interchange coming through you maybe don't know about.

DAN
I know all about it; the site is archaeologically too important to be superseded by—

CHAD
(*Overlapping from "to be superseded"*)

They may be hot shit to you; Dad and me don't happen
to want our property—

DAN
You don't realize how important a man like August Howe
is. Jesus Christ, you talk like—

CHAD
—My land, baby! MY LAND! MY LAND! It don't belong to
your Indian god. It don't belong to you. It's my land and
there is an Interstate coming through. Now, if you want
to sit in its way, every one of you, good, you're invited.

KIRSTEN
The Interstate isn't coming through your land.

AUGUST
That isn't necessary now.

CHAD
Hell, it isn't. You think they're going to build a motel
where there isn't a highway?

DAN
(Overlapping from "where there")
Then they won't build it. What the hell difference does it
make? You're talking about a goddamn Holiday Inn.

CHAD
They been here! I've seen the plans!

DAN
Goddamnit, there's a law since 1954—in this state—against
public-funded construction defacing Indian monuments.

CHAD
(Beat.)

Well, guys, I hate to disappoint you, but you're thinking about it a little late.

DAN

We thought about it two years ago. (*Pause.*) When did you last hear from your motel architects?

CHAD

What do you mean, two years ago?

DAN

Professor Howe prepared a—

AUGUST

—Not tonight. In the morning—

DAN

(*Right over*)
—August prepared a report to the legislature on the importance of this site—

CHAD

—Well, I'm sorry he went to all the trouble—

DAN

The highway isn't going to be anywhere near Blue Shoals. It's been rerouted to the other side of the goddamn lake! We got notice before we came down this summer.

(*A long pause.*)

CYNTHIA

When was this, August?

CHAD

Shit. "When"—Let on like—

DAN

Two years; after our first summer; after we heard about the highway.

CYNTHIA

It must have been a lot of trouble keeping me in the dark.

DELIA

We're a bad risk, Cynthia.

AUGUST

It was a matter of a brief report, a few pictures, and a phone call.

JEAN

You can't do that.

DAN

Old man Jasker wouldn't allow the land to become a national monument. How else could we protect them?

CYNTHIA

Them? Protect them or protect you?

CHAD

Boy, you're pretending to be my friend; you're listening to me talking about soul food and grilled bass out of the lake; what are you saying behind my back? Leading me on. Where do you get off thinking you're better than the people around here and can take over and take away everything we hope for—where—laughing about my goddamned island—what do you care. Millions! You're trying to steal from me!

JEAN

You don't know what it meant to him.

DAN

I know what it means to me; you should know what it means to me.

CYNTHIA

Using my photographs of the dig to surreptitiously—

DAN

Chad, I'm trying to make you see that you'd be better off —understand the value of what you have here, God, the place—

CHAD

(*A howling scream.*)
NOOOOOOOOO! (*Silence. A pained plea*) How can you treat people . . . ?

(*Pause.*)

JEAN

Chad. I went down to the courthouse; I saw the model you told me to see, I . . .

CHAD

(*Fiercely to* AUGUST)
—you won't get it. I know what you want, Professor, but you might just have to stay up at State next summer with your whore and fuck her yourself.
(*He exits.*)

CYNTHIA

Chad? (*Going out.*) Jasker, goddamnit, stay here. Talk to me! I didn't know.

DAN

What model at the courthouse?

JEAN

Of the motel and the resort; it isn't important.

DELIA

I may take you up, Dan, on writing that book.

AUGUST

I'm glad you're walking; I don't think it's necessary for
you to stay.

DELIA

Not at all. Cynthia said Jasker'd be ripped off— I guess—

AUGUST

If I thought it were possible for you to write, I'd ad-
monish against it.

DELIA

You always have. I never needed either your approval or
"admonishments"; Dad respected what I was doing, that
was enough for me.

AUGUST

What you never realized was that Dad and I were close.
You didn't want us to be, so you supposed it to be the way
you wanted.

DELIA

(Overlapping on "you supposed")
—I was never interested in your opinion of anything I
was—

AUGUST

—Thinking you were some kind of *Wunderkind* and assuming—

DELIA
—He respected what I was doing and that was—

AUGUST
—Dad never read a word you wrote. He quoted your reviews back to you verbatim and laughed behind your back because you never noticed. He thought you were a fool.

CYNTHIA
(*Re-enters, goes upstairs.*)
Come upstairs, Kirsten; come to bed.

AUGUST
(*To them*)
Dan, it's late, I hadn't thought we'd sleep much tonight, but maybe that's the best thing to do. We'll be getting up at five.
(*Leaving.*)

DELIA
Dad's opinion was always too important to me. Thank you.

AUGUST
You're welcome.

(*He is gone, so is* DELIA; *the others begin to leave as the night sounds increase, along with a weirdly close screech owl, and the lights fade as tractor sounds are heard. As the stage becomes dark, we can hear someone moving about.*)

DAN'S VOICE
Hello? Jesus Christ. Is somebody down there? (*Pause. Flashlight.*) Delia? Hello?

(*The beam catches* CHAD *full in the face. He is wearing the God-King's mask, and has the knapsack in his arms. He stands perfectly still.*)

CHAD
The light's in my face.

DAN
(*The beam from the flashlight moves to* CHAD's *loaded arms.* DAN *stays on the stairs.*)
Chad?

CHAD
Cynthia said you was a light sleeper.

(*Pause.*)

DAN
Yeah.

CHAD
I got something I want to show you.

(*Pause.*)

DAN
You . . . shouldn't handle . . .

(*Pause.*)

CHAD
It's only copper. They treasured it higher than gold.

DAN
What have you got in—what are you doing?

CHAD
There's something outside I want to show you.

DAN
What?

CHAD
Come outside.
(*He moves to the door.*)

DAN
Don't go out with that . . .

CHAD
There's something I want to show you.

DAN
Chad? (*The light plays across the empty table.*) Chad?
(*Back to the door through which* CHAD *has disappeared outside.*)

CHAD
(*Off*)
I want to show you something.

(DAN *moves down the stairs and out.*

As a slow dawn begins, a girl's voice is heard calling, "Dr. Loggins?" Repeatedly, then another girl calling the same. AUGUST, *barely awake, stumbles down, buckling his belt, yells out the window, "Yes, goddamnit," and goes off.* KIRSTEN *follows him almost immediately, but stops at the bottom of the stairs as* DELIA, *fully dressed, enters.*)

KIRSTEN
(*Sullen*)
Good morning.

DELIA
Good morning.

(KIRSTEN *goes out as* DELIA *takes a bottle of tonic from the refrigerator.*)

JEAN
(*Entering.*)
My God, real clothes.

DELIA
The better to leave your enclave.

(*The light continues to intensify.*)

JEAN
Oh. Well, I guess you know what you need. Did Pollyandy sleep down here last night or did he even get home?

DELIA
I don't know.

JEAN
I woke up; then I managed to get pissed off enough to go back to sleep. He said something about celebrating the God-King's discovery with a mescaline trip, but I think he was blithering.

DELIA
Where would anyone get mescaline in Blue Shoals, Illinois?

JEAN
You've been away longer than you know. (*Going out.*) It's gorgeous out.

(*There are a few noises, girls' voices,* AUGUST's.)

CYNTHIA
(*Off*)
What? (*Muffled answer.*) I'll be down— Said, I'll be down.
(*She appears.*) The son of a bitch. I'll kill him.

DELIA
You'll kill whom?

AUGUST
(*Off*)
It's mad— He's a madman, it's crazy—

JEAN
(*Off*)
August, where is—

AUGUST
(*Entering.*)
Not now, damnit; not now.

CYNTHIA
Chad Jasker.

AUGUST
Everything's gone. He's carried everything off—the bulldozer's been run over the site—the bulldozer is out in the
lake in six feet of water, apparently where it got stuck—

(CYNTHIA *goes out.*)

DELIA
Is Dan out there?

AUGUST
What's to do? There's nothing to do. Let him sleep it off.

KIRSTEN
(*Entering.*)

The girls are calling you.

DELIA
(*As* JEAN *enters*)
Jean, you'd better go in and call the county sheriff.

JEAN
Tell him he's wrecked the site.

DELIA
Tell him Dan is missing.

(JEAN *stands transfixed for a second. Turns and goes into the office.*)

AUGUST
Oh, God, no.

CYNTHIA
(*Entering.*)
I tried to tell August he didn't know what he was dealing with.

AUGUST
Cynthia—I want you to sit down.
(*Takes her hands.*)

CYNTHIA
What? (*Breaks away.*) Oh, please.

AUGUST
Please.

CYNTHIA
What? What is it? Don't hold on to me, you know I don't like to be grabbed at. What on earth . . . (*Freeze. Looks around.*) He's left. He's run off . . .

AUGUST
No, no, no, no . . .

CYNTHIA
Where?

AUGUST
There's the possibility that—

CYNTHIA
Oh, damn your possibilities—

AUGUST
Dan hasn't— Dan isn't here. Did you talk to Jasker last
night?

DELIA
Did he tell you anything?

CYNTHIA
I couldn't find him.

DELIA
What is Jasker capable of? I never looked at him twice until last night.

CYNTHIA
He'd do anything.

DELIA
You know what I'm talking about; I want to know if the
madman is capable—

CYNTHIA
—Yes, yes! He's capable of anything—

DELIA
He hurt you; you know.

CYNTHIA
—Yes, repeatedly. Yes. (DELIA *exits. Pause.*) You didn't tell me about the highway because you knew I'd tell him. I would have.

AUGUST
What matters is finding Dan.

CYNTHIA
We have nothing to show for our dig, August. We have nine pictures I took last night.

AUGUST
I know.

CYNTHIA
The little bastard thought he wiped us out completely, but we fooled him.

AUGUST
That isn't important to me.

CYNTHIA
What a stupid thing to lie about. (*As* AUGUST *starts to move away*) Well, I can do one thing for him.
(*Takes up the camera, ejects the film, and begins unrolling it.*)

AUGUST
Stop it! CYNTHIA!

CYNTHIA
(*Throwing the unrolled film on the floor as he reaches her.*)
There! I can do that much for him. There's your evidence.

JEAN
(*Entering.*)
There are two police cars turning into the field if you want
to go out. I'm trying to think where they might have . . .

(*The light immediately confines* AUGUST *to his desk area.*)

AUGUST
At eleven that morning an oar from Chad Jasker's boat was
found floating near the center of the lake. At nine that
night townspeople turned their car headlights out across
the water to assist the divers who had come down from
Marion.

(*Car headlights swing across the room.* DELIA *turns on a
lamp.*)

JEAN
Where the hell are all the people coming from? Why don't
they stay away?

CYNTHIA
People from town, volunteers; there's almost no police
force.

KIRSTEN
They've got men with diving equipment.

JEAN
I can't help; I can't go outside; I'm swamped with com-
miserations. Keep those damn girls out of here; keep them
all out.

CYNTHIA
August does that. They know better than to come here.

DELIA
Who's the old man?

CYNTHIA
Old man Jasker.

DELIA
What are all the goddamned people doing here; the cars
keep turning into the area, there must be fifty cars.

CYNTHIA
They see the lights, they think we've discovered something.

DELIA
Can't they keep them away?

CYNTHIA
There's no law.

DELIA
All the laws are the wrong goddamned laws.

CYNTHIA
Someone heard we had discovered a monster in the lake.
The sightseers will go away; the men will work all night.

KIRSTEN
They've got a lot of machinery for a small town.

JEAN
(*Running to the screen door.*)
THEY ARE NOT TO DRAG THE LAKE. THEY USE GRAPPLING
HOOKS TO DRAG THE LAKE. THEY ARE NOT TO DRAG THE LAKE!
They said they'd send for divers!

DELIA
Shut up!

JEAN

I'm going to be fine.

DELIA

You can't help. Shut up.

JEAN

Why did he go out? Why didn't someone hear him? Why did the girls stay at the motel? WHY DID HE HAVE TO HEAR NOISES IN THE NIGHT? WHY DID HE TRUST PEOPLE, WHY DID HE BELIEVE IN THINGS? (DELIA *slaps her across the face. Holds her a moment.* JEAN *sits.* DELIA *sits beside her.*) Morbid, morbid, stupid people. Vanished without a trace. I'm going to be fine. Cochise. Co-C-O-co. Vanished without a trace. I want the bone awl. I want the—

CYNTHIA

(*Going to her.*)

Jean, please. Please. We don't have it. It's gone.

AUGUST

Dianne, Dianne . . . We left the house for the last time August 8. I went back in January, only hoping to see the lake take it away. In my mind's eye the river's currents swept the house before it as a great brown flood bears off everything in its path. That was in my mind's eye. The lake had risen to half-cover the house. Much of the second level was above the water. The house looked more scuttled than inundated. The lake rises as a great long hand-shaped pond, slowly . . .

(*Stops, turns the machine off. The women hardly move.* CYNTHIA *stares off,* JEAN *sits, her head in* DELIA's *lap.*)

CYNTHIA

August won't work without Dan.

JEAN
Does it matter?

CYNTHIA
No.

DELIA
Yes. Of course it does.

CYNTHIA
He doesn't know he won't work.

DELIA
Yes, he does.

JEAN
(*Not moving.*)
I'm too heavy on you.

DELIA
You weigh nothing.

JEAN
Are they gone?

DELIA
The divers will be back at nine.

CYNTHIA
They won't find them.

DELIA
Shhhh.

CYNTHIA
They won't find them.

DELIA
Shhhh.

CYNTHIA
They won't.

DELIA
Shhhh.

CYNTHIA
They won't find them.

(AUGUST *presses the tape recorder. It plays.*)

TAPE
. . . to see the lake take it away. In my mind's eye the river's currents swept the house before it as a great brown flood bears off everything in its path. That was in my mind's eye. The lake had risen to half-cover the house. Much of the second level was above the water. The house looked more scuttled than inundated. The lake rises as a great long hand-shaped pond, slowly . . .

(*He turns the machine off a second, then turns it on.*)

AUGUST
Dianne . . . (*Turns machine off. After a moment he turns it on.*) Dianne . . .

(*The women fade.* AUGUST *tries to frame a statement. The machine continues to record the stillness.* AUGUST *stands with the mike in his hand, very still. The tape continues to turn. A long pause. The lights fade on him.*)

CURTAIN